SHORT TIME'S ENDLESS MONUMENT

One day I wrote her name upon the strand,
  but came the waves and washed it away:
  agayne I wrote it with a second hand,
  but came the tyde, and made my paynes his pray.
Vayne man, sayd she, that doest in vaine assay,
  a mortall thing so to immortalize,
  for I my selve shall lyke to this decay,
  and eek my name bee wyped out lykewize.
Not so, (quod I) let baser things devize
  to dy in dust, but you shall live by fame:
  my verse your vertues rare shall eternize,
  and in the hevens wryte your glorious name.
Where whenas death shall all the world subdew,
  our love shall live, and later life renew.

                              (*Amoretti* 75)

SHORT TIME'S
ENDLESS MONUMENT

The symbolism of the numbers in
Edmund Spenser's *Epithalamion*

by A. Kent Hieatt

KENNIKAT PRESS
Port Washington, N. Y./London

SHORT TIME'S ENDLESS MONUMENT

Manufactured by Taylor Publishing Company   Dallas, Texas

For Constance

> . . . εἰκὼ δ'ἐπενόει κινητόν τινα αἰῶνος ποιῆσαι,
> καὶ διακοσμῶν ἅμα οὐρανὸν ποιεῖ μένοντος αἰῶνος
> ἐν ἑνὶ κατ' ἀριθμὸν ἰοῦσαν αἰώνιον εἰκόνα, τοῦτον
> ὅν δὴ χρόνον ὠνομάκαμεν.
>
> *Timaeus* 37d

> Horchet! horcht! Dem Sturm der Horen
> Tönend wird für Geistes-Ohren
> Schon der neue Tag geboren.
> Felsenthore knarren rasselnd,
> Phöbus Räder rollen prasselnd,
> Welch Getöse bringt das Licht!
> Es trommetet, es posaunet,
> Auge blinzt und Ohr erstaunet,
> Unerhörtes hört sich nicht.
> Schlüpfet zu den Blumenkronen,
> Tiefer, tiefer, still zu wohnen,
> In die Felsen, unter's Laub;
> Trifft es euch, so seid ihr taub.
>
> *Faust,* 4666–78

> So let us rest, sweet love, in hope of this,
> And cease till then our tymely joyes to sing,
> The woods no more us answer, nor our eccho ring.
>
> *Epithalamion,* 424–26

ACKNOWLEDGMENTS

A number of colleagues and friends lent their aid to the exercise in literary detection upon which this book is based. Professor William Nelson read part of the work in progress and on a number of points made suggestions that turned out to be just the right ones. Professor Josephine Waters Bennett and Professor Andrew Chiappe later read the complete manuscript and helped me with several details. Professor Jan Schilt and Professor Isadore Epstein were kindly authorities in astronomical matters. In various ways Professor Richard Chase, Professor Thomas Flanagan, Professor Howard Schless, Professor Mark Van Doren, and Mr. James Zito expedited my task, and a number of students (some of whom are named in the notes) patiently sat through extended disquisitions and offered suggestions. The staff of Columbia University Press, particularly in the person of Miss Elisabeth L. Shoemaker, have been most courteously and efficiently helpful. The Johns Hopkins Press has kindly permitted me to reproduce the text of *Epithalamion* from *The Works of Edmund Spenser: A Variorum Edition*.

To all of them, and to others, my thanks go out. In the matter of my wife both the usual words and others fail me. Her name appears in the dedication, as it does (in slightly altered form) at the head of the seventh book of *The Faerie Queene*, where its relation to Mutability may be equated with that of the sun and the other stars.

CONTENTS

Errata

P. 12, *line* 33 *for* Conclusion *read* "Conclusion"
P. 46, *line* 26 *for* approximate *read* approximately
P. 98, *line* 8 *for* they *read* thy

SHORT TIME'S ENDLESS MONUMENT

INTRODUCTION

To looke upon a worke of rare devise
The which a workman setteth out to view,
And not to yield it the deserved prise,
That unto such a workmanship is dew,
   Doth either prove the judgement to be naught
   Or els doth shew a mind with envy fraught.

        . . .

And thus I hang a garland at the dore,
Not for to shew the goodness of the ware:
But such hath beene the custome heretofore,
And customes very hardly broken are.
   And when your tast shall tell you this is trew,
   Then looke you give your hoast his utmost dew.
(Ignoto. From Commendatory Verses to *The Faerie Queene*)

What this book attempts to show is the presence of a dominant, most surprising, and hitherto unsuspected symbolic structure and meaning in a marriage ode generally known as one of the dozen or so great poems of our language. My purpose in the first [1] and second chapters below, and in a text of Spenser's *Epithalamion* with glosses, is to point out certain previously unnoticed peculiarities of the poem which clearly call for explanation. An interpretation is given in Chapters III and IV; the Conclusion considers allied matters.

In a journalistic sense the facts and interpretations presented here are novel—in fact, staggering: they appear to have gone unnoticed for 365 years; they suggest something apparently un-

---

[1] The material of the first chapter was scheduled for publication in *Modern Language Notes* in 1960. It was withdrawn when it became evident that the present book would be published in the same year.

precedented among all the other great lyrics of world literature. They matter rather more, however, in their significance for the history of Renaissance poetic symbolism and for our understanding of Spenser. But they are most important as they affect our estimate of a great poem which is known far and wide, as others of Spenser's poems (rightly or wrongly) are not. It follows that this book should engage the attention of many whose first interest is not Spenser and the Elizabethans, and who are usually interested in studies of Spenser only for their bearing on general questions of poetic expression. But it is necessary to concentrate the present discussion on the assessment of objective data and on demonstrating that Spenser used certain symbolic devices for definite purposes in *Epithalamion,* rather than on the nature of the poetic achievement conditioned by these. It is not, in the first place, so much a question of whether a new and possibly fruitful way of looking at Spenser's poetry has been discovered, as it is of whether Spenser himself quite consciously intended to do the surprising thing which is here described; that is to say, the problem must be historical before it can become aesthetic, because, in a poem at so great a distance from us and of such complexity, we must be particularly sure of what we are looking at before we decide what we think of it.

The fact remains that most readers of *Epithalamion* are bound to consider the importance of this discovery for the study of Renaissance literary symbolism and of Spenser as secondary to the question of its impact upon the reputation of the poem itself. It therefore seems appropriate, before embarking on the demonstration, to say something briefly and tentatively on this subject.

Among all Spenser's works, *Epithalamion* seems today to be almost the only one possessing a poetic resonance validating it immediately for the reader who comes to Spenser only with some understanding of poetry, as against the man who is fortunate enough, or who has taken enough trouble, to possess Spenser's world partly as his own. Its "festal sublimity" (in the words of Professor C. S. Lewis), its maintenance of tone, its effortless—apparently almost unconscious—fusion of the mythological and the sacred with the telling details from daily life, its masterfully original deployment of the materials of an immemorial epithalamial tradition—all these combine to make it a compelling and commanding poem. Perhaps its main achievement has seemed to most readers to lie in the impression it gives of freshness and effortless ease. This impression springs, apparently, not only from Spenser's decorous skill, but also from the joyous import for him of the occasion, which was not simply one instance *tout court* of the institution and sacrament of marriage (important as that was to his conception of love and of human continuity), but his own marriage, at about forty years of age, after a long and arduous courtship, to Elizabeth Boyle, who was presumably in her twenties.

In the light of the present thesis, however, these good reasons for admiring *Epithalamion* must form part of a much larger view if they are to remain reasons at all. In this new picture of the poem one imperative given by the Renaissance ideal of *sprezzatura* —that in all action there must be effortless ease and grace of performance—must be supplemented by the other, which is that the action itself should be something supremely important, difficult, and indeed seemingly miraculous. This miracle, if miracle it be, is my concern in this book: not the poem as we have all known it, but an unexpected, very complex, and highly integrated symbolism which underlies the literal meaning just as allegorical meanings underlie the literal surface of *The Faerie Queene*, although in this case the symbolism is carried through by quite different devices from those in the longer work. The significance of this symbolism, if I have understood it correctly, relates *Epithalamion* much more intimately than has been previously seen to ideas expressed elsewhere in Spenser's works—in the Gardens of Adonis and Venus, in Nature's judgment of Mutability, and elsewhere in *The Faerie Queene,* and in his *Hymns*—and to matters expressed in the work of Spenser's predecessor Chaucer and that of a long line of medieval poets. Understanding of this symbolism requires at least some knowledge of the geography and values of a particular medieval-Renaissance world-view which can be entertained today only in a highly modified and intellectualized form, and which is, in large part, entertained in much more restricted circles than it used to be. Yet, if the validity of this interpretation is granted, no intelligent reading of *Epithalamion* can be accomplished without a grasp of this symbolism, because it is so strongly woven into the substance of the poem and because it is so important to the total effect.

It is hard to say what this may mean for the reputation of a great poem. When all is said and done, Spenser's method, in which Milton follows him, is a traditional medieval and Renaissance one, although worked out in this ode in what appears to be a highly original way. This method requires that beneath a simple literal surface profound symbolic communication of an integrated continuity should take place covertly, but in a way that will reveal itself to the intelligent and sympathetic reader; and this is not so very different from the method, recognized or not, of many literary works at the present time. But what many modern readers object to in this method as Spenser employs it (they object to much else about his poetry, partly with justice) can be best understood by remembering how strongly it contrasts with the method of a Metaphysical poet like Donne, however similar his and Spenser's poetic aims may finally be. Given enough knowledge and close reading, a poem of Donne's yields up its meaning gradually but easily because the explicit complexity at the literal surface, not something working away complexly in its interior, leads one to this meaning: a perusal of *A Nocturnal upon St. Lucy's Day* (having as its point of departure the shortest day in the year as *Epithalamion* has the longest one) will show the reader, after he has finished this book, what I mean. It is this kind of complexity, despite the presently declining reputation of Donne's poetry, which rightly attracts attention at once; the other kind arouses (I think wrongly) a complex of antagonisms, in which horror of the learned explicator plays no small part, but of which the largest item is probably this view: that to appreciate such an integrated symbolism of meaning as that of *Epithalamion,* proceeding on a line parallel with the literal one, but not constantly and intimately generated by it, requires an act of the will, not of the imagination—that this symbolism is calculated and constricting, not liberating, for meaning. But to make such a complaint is both to lose sight of one way in which the imagination may work, and to rely on a false estimate of the development of Renaissance poetry. We have largely lost the habit of deriving aesthetic pleasure from reading a sustained and integrated expression of poetic meaning on two levels (as Professor C. S. Lewis does not tire of telling us), and we neglect the fact that Donne's poetry is just as "calculated" as the best of Spenser's is (as Professor Rosemond Tuve similarly tells us), even if it is made to seem more opportunistic and flexible.

One must leave out of the picture temporarily those readers who are more interested in the shock and apparent irreverence towards established views to be found in Donne's early poetry than they are in the sobriety of ultimate commitment (Donne's or anyone's else)—who, in other words, are not interested in what Spenser has to say. But I believe that once another kind of reader has found out what Spenser is really after in *Epithalamion* he can experience that meaning poetically for what it is—an act of empathy with, and affirmation of, life and the world, insofar as these, in spite of everything, can be finally affirmed.

I. THE STANZAS AND THE LONG LINES

> Needes must he all eternitie survive,
> That can to other give eternall dayes.
> (from Spenser's envoy to his *Ruines of Rome: by Bellay*)

Certain peculiarities in *Epithalamion* go to make up a puzzling pattern. None of these features of Spenser's great marriage ode seems significant when taken singly; their total impact, however, strongly suggests the presence of a hitherto neglected symbolic pattern underlying the poem. Four of the peculiarities, some well known and some not, are treated in the present chapter.

The first of these is that the bride in *Epithalamion* is attended by the Hours, as no other character is among the myriads attended by deities or personifications in all the rest of Spenser's known work:

> But first come ye fayre houres which were begot
> In Joves sweet paradice, of Day and Night,
> Which doe the seasons of the year allot,
> And al that ever in this world is fayre
> Doe make and still repayre.[1]

(98–102)

Furthermore, as appears from the lines above, these Hours are not only the daily ones we know, but also the representatives or deities of the seasons of the year, like the *Horae* of classical antiquity, and they are credited with creative and restorative functions.

---

[1] All quotations from Spenser follow the text of the Variorum edition, except that *i*, *u*, and *v* are normalized.

The second peculiarity is this: *Epithalamion* is the only one of Spenser's numerous verse works in which the lengths, rime schemes, and metrical structure of the stanzas vary freely. Typically, the *Epithalamion* stanza (of which there are twenty-three followed by a short envoy) is made up of four groups of long lines—pentameters and a concluding hexameter—among which are interpolated three short lines—trimeters in all but two cases.[2] But the number of lines in the groups of long lines varies, and in two of the regular stanzas (beginning at l. 261 and l. 409) there are only two short lines per stanza, not three, in all editions. As a result the regular stanzas vary in length from seventeen to nineteen lines.

These variations have usually been explained as an effect of expressive freedom, or of Spenser's desire to follow the form of the Italian *canzone,* although no *canzone* he is likely to have read comes anywhere near the length of *Epithalamion,* and the similar stanzas of *Prothalamion,* a poem associated with this one by date and genre, do not vary at all in length, metrical structure, or rime scheme. Spenser may indeed have been (in fact, probably was) trying to obtain the effect suggested by these explanations, but he may also have had a more important reason for varying the number of long and short lines per stanza. This reason follows from the fourth of the peculiarities, to be noted below; in accordance with it, he could not have obtained his end without this variation unique in his works.

The third and fourth peculiar features of the poem are of a quite different nature from the first two. They are strictly interdependent, and the conclusions derived from them, buttressed by the two points above, can be appreciated only in relation to each other.

In the third place, then, *Epithalamion* contains twenty-four stanzas—twenty-three long ones plus a short envoy. It is possible

2 Lines 16 and 431 are tetrameters.

that by this feature of ¹ˑ   ⸝em Spenser alludes to the twenty-four
hours of the day, and specifically to the hours of his marriage day
—the summer solstice or longest day in the year, as it is indicated
to be in the poem (l. 265). Two grounds for supposing that the
number of stanzas forms such an allusion, and is not in fact coin-
cidental, are (1) another likely calendrical reference, discussed as
the fourth feature below, and (2) a particular division which
Spenser has made among his twenty-four stanzas.

This division has to do with the hours of light and darkness on
the poet's marriage day. The action of the poem appears to begin,
within vague limits, just before sunrise (l. 19) and to end some
time before the next sunrise. The stanzas devoted to the day are
set off from those of the night by a change of refrain: up to stanza
17, in which night falls, the refrains are positive, on the general
pattern, "The woods shall to me answer and my Eccho ring."
From stanza 17 down to the envoy, the refrains are negative, on
the general pattern, "The woods no more shal answere, nor your
echo ring."

On the day of the wedding (the longest in the year) and in
the latitudes in southern Ireland where the marriage took place,
the number of hours of daylight is sixteen and a fraction [3]—a
circumstance Spenser could have learned from a variety of sources.
On the assumption that the twenty-four stanzas of the poem are
an allusion to the hours of his marriage day, the sixteen and a
fraction stanzas down to the arrival of night and the seven and a
fraction succeeding stanzas would be equally an allusion to the
hours of daylight and of darkness on the same day, and the allusion would be underlined by the use of positive and negative refrains. It was, of course, a common practice, in Spenser's time as
long before, to count the twenty-four hours of the day from sunrise.

[3] The fraction is between forty-five and forty-nine minutes for Castle
Kilcolman, Cork, and Youghal. I am indebted to Professor Jan Schilt for
this information, on the basis of latitudes provided by me.

Here again, the possibility of coincidence is not to be discounted in the appearance of these numbers, but a further datum seriously weakens the possibility.

The datum has to be arrived at in a somewhat roundabout way. In *The Kalender of Sheperdes*,[4] with which Spenser was surely familiar, and in Johannes de Sacrobosco's highly popular *De sphaera*,[5] the hours of daylight on the longest day of the year are given as sixteen and one quarter for the northern edge of the seventh "clime," which is the nearest latitude to southern Ireland of all those for which figures are given in both works. Now, the seventeenth stanza of *Epithalamion*, in which night arrives, is divided, like most of the other stanzas, into four groups of long lines (pentameters and one concluding hexameter) by the interpolation of three short lines (trimeters), giving the special music by which the *Epithalamion*-stanza is known. Night falls at l. 300, precisely at the end of the first of the four groups of long lines, as indicated by my italics:

> Now ceasse ye damsels your delights forepast;
> Enough it is, that all the day was youres:
> Now day is doen, and night is nighing fast:
> *Now night is come*, now soone her disaray,
> And in her bed her lay.

This first group of long lines (to which I have added the following short one) is thus devoted to day, until its concluding lines,

[4] Edited by H. O. Sommer (London, 1892), II, iv verso. This is the 1503 edition. The 1506 edition, also edited by Sommer, misplaces the figures (III, 135, l. 2, and 134, ll. 15–17). The value appears in its correct place in an edition thought to be of 1570: *The Shepardes Kalender . . . Imprinted by T. Este for J. Wally* (University Microfilms No. 17939, S. T. C. No. 22415), kiiii. It appears correctly in all French editions I have consulted.

[5] *The* Sphere *of Sacrobosco and its Commentators* (ed. Lynn Thorndike, Chicago, 1949), p. 140. The northern edge of the seventh clime, said by Sacrobosco and the *Kalender* to be the northernmost inhabitable region, is actually in the latitude of Devon.

and the remaining three of the four groups of long lines are given over to night, concluding with the first of the negative refrains. The hypothesis to which I wish to draw attention here is that the first of these four groups in this seventeenth stanza is being made equivalent to the fraction in the figure of sixteen and one quarter already mentioned, and that the three remaining groups are similarly being made equivalent to the fraction in the figure of seven and three quarters for the hours of night on this longest day in the year, according to *De sphaera* and the *Kalender*.

In point of fact it is not necessary to push this theory here; all that is needed at present is that we should use it as an assumption for purposes of argument so as to arrive at a particular datum. But of the theory itself it must be said that it at first seems over-subtle, particularly since from it would seem to follow that Spenser carried his symbolism to the somewhat extraordinary point of indicating quarter-hourly divisions in his (putative) stanza hours by marking these divisions with short lines. The hypothesis also suggests a further subtlety: that the long lines are symbolic equivalents of the duration of time (i.e., here, a quarter hour for each group), and the short ones of divisions of time (i.e., marking at three places the subdivisions of the stanza into four parts). All of this may appear difficult to accept; yet there is one reason for supposing that the long lines, at least, symbolize duration of time in quite a different sense. This—the fourth of the peculiarities alluded to above—is that the total number of such long lines in the poem is 365.

It may, then, be suggested (although not positively affirmed) that by this feature of the poem Spenser alludes to the days of the year, as he may allude to the hours of the day in the twenty-four stanzas.

The main difficulty with this suggestion is that it is unprecedented: although Spenser's occasional minor preoccupation with considerations of numerical symmetry has been noticed (see Conclusion, below), no Renaissance poem has been convincingly shown (to my knowledge) to possess such extensive numerological symbolism as this. Yet the facts outlined above form so strong a pattern that the suggestion cannot be lightly dismissed. First, there are the numbers themselves: the number of stanzas corresponds to the number of hours in the day; their division into two classes by refrains corresponds to the division between light and darkness on the day and in the place of the marriage described in the poem; the number of long lines corresponds to the number of days in the year. It is true that the appearance of the totals 24, 16-odd, and 365 might in itself be adventitious, but there are two other reasons for believing it is not.

In the first place, if (according to the supposition here expressed) Spenser decided at some point in the gestation of his poem that it should contain just twenty-four stanzas and exactly 365 long lines, he would then have found himself faced with the necessity of doing something that he did at no other place in his published works: he would have had to vary his stanzaic lengths without apparent reason. It is arithmetically impossible for a poem containing 365 lines of a certain description to be divided into twenty-four stanzas each containing the same number of such lines. The number of such lines per stanza must vary. It may be granted that the envoy of such a poem might in any case be shorter than any of the other stanzas, but the result, arithmetically, is the same: the number of long lines per stanza in the other twenty-three stanzas must vary, even if the envoy be allowed to occupy any number of lines, up to the size of any of the other stanzas. Now, in point of fact, Spenser did vary his stanzaic lengths freely, without apparent reason, in *Epithalamion,* and he did this in no other poem. In fact, considering that there are six long lines in the envoy, the long lines are distributed among the remaining stanzas as evenly as they can be, on the premise that the total aimed at, with the envoy's six long lines, was 365. Fourteen of these remaining stanzas contain sixteen long lines each; nine contain fifteen long lines each. All of this goes to support further the theory that Spenser was aiming specifically at 365 long lines in twenty-four stanzas, presumably with symbolic purposes having to do with the day and the year.

A second reason for supposing that the arithmetical totals are not adventitious is the following: if Spenser intended to write a poem alluding through its form to the hours of the day and the days of the year, he would probably be concerned with some diurnal and annual significance in his subject matter. And, in fact, the Hours are the first attendants upon the bride, in their significance both as hours of the day and as seasons of the year. We have already pointed out that the Hours attend no one in the rest of Spenser's known poetry. This particular allusion, by means of the Hours, to the day and the year in *Epithalamion* is not the clearest verbal one, which, in context, is probably

> But for this time it ill ordained was,
> To chose the longest day in all the yeare,
> And shortest night, when longest fitter weare . . .

> (270–72)

But, because of its exceptional character in Spenser's works, it is the one which lends the strongest verbal support to the theory that the course of *Epithalamion* corresponds symbolically in one way to the passage of a day, and in another way to that of a year.

If we do not accept this theory as a working hypothesis, we must assume that nothing but coincidence is involved in the apparent convergence of no fewer than five separate circumstances of the poem: i.e., the three correspondences of numerical totals to chronological ones, and the two Spenserian anomalies of free stanzaic variation and attendance upon a character by the Hours. If the theory is accepted, however, the convergence is explained. Consequently it seems safer to put our trust provisionally in this theory as a point of departure than to reject it out of hand. That is all that is needed at this stage.

Admittedly, the hypothesis raises as many questions as it answers. In particular, what would Spenser's purpose have been in alluding not simply to the day of the summer solstice, but also to the year, in a poem on a marriage day? And why, for instance, did he vary the number of short lines per stanza, as well as the long ones? Neither of these problems, nor any of the others that might be raised, can be profitably approached until we have considered another aspect of the poem. Before doing so, however, it will be well to return to one point. The division of long lines among the first twenty-three stanzas of the poem is as even as possible, as though considerations of symmetry had dictated their allotment. But we do not yet know on what grounds Spenser assigned just six long lines to his envoy. Certainly nothing about this stanza suggests that Spenser had a reason for his choice in either personal habit or tradition, for neither the stanzaic form, with its six long and one short lines, nor the rime scheme (ababacc) is employed elsewhere in his work, nor does the stanza correspond to any familiar form of Renaissance poetry. It may be, of course, that the length of the envoy was dictated solely by the length of what Spenser had to say. Yet nowhere else do we find him unsuccessful in tailoring what he wishes to express to the exigencies of a pre-established stanza. He may not always do this well, but he does it. The apparent anomaly thus remains.

II. THE MATCHING STANZAS

> During the which there was an heavenly noise
> Heard sound through all the Pallace pleasantly,
> Like as it had bene many an Angels voice,
> Singing before th'eternall majesty,
> In their trinall triplicities on hye;
> Yet wist no creature, whence that heavenly sweet
> Proceeded, yet eachone felt secretly
> Himself thereby reft of his sences meet,
> And ravished with rare impression in his sprite.
> (the betrothal of Una and Redcross, *Faerie Queene* 1.12.39)

A further peculiarity of *Epithalamion* is that stanzas at some distance from each other in the poem contain elements which seem to pair, or match each other, in various ways, but generally in the form of conceits. Some of these pairings are more obvious than others. Stanza 9 and stanza 21, for instance, plainly contain two such elements. In stanza 9 the bride is said to come forth as does Phoebe, the moon-goddess, when she rises in the east, prepared "to run her mighty race" through the heavens. The bride is then described in terms applicable in part to the moon, and she is said to seem "lyke some mayden Queene." In stanza 21 the moon herself, identified as Cynthia, looks in the window and is described as one who "walks about high heaven al the night." There follows the long-recognized allusion [1] to the Virgin Queen, Elizabeth I.

Another pair of stanzas, 10 and 22, respectively succeeding the stanzas just described, also resemble each other, though not so obviously. They are both concerned with things physical. Stanza

[1] An excuse to her for loving another, after the pattern of *Amoretti* 80 and *Faerie Queene* 6.10.28. Cf. Variorum note.

10 describes the bride's physical glories; stanza 22 is a prayer for issue in the physical sense of conception on the wedding night, through the secret succoring of the pleasures of love. Just beyond these stanzas, 11 and 23 show a similar resemblance: stanza 11 deals with the spiritual excellences of the bride, describes them as "heavenly" and "celestial," and contrasts them with her physical beauty on the score that the spiritual is invisible. Stanza 23, on the other hand, is an appeal for spiritual excellence in the offspring of the marriage. The appeal is directed both to the high heavens, which lend light to wretched men, and to the invisible powers which reside there: on all these counts the similarities are patent.

The appearance of pairing continues in stanzas 12 and 24: for one thing, the words "due" and "endless" appear in both these stanzas and nowhere else in the poem; for another, the ways in which the words are applied are parallel. In stanza 12 the poet commands that the temple gates be opened wide, that the gateposts be "adorned," and that the pillars be "decked" so as to receive the bride ("this Saynt") with honor *"dew."* The word similarly applies in stanza 24 to what is "due" the bride. His bride should *"duly"* have been "decked" with many "ornaments" and the song honoring her has not come at its *"dew* time." Similarly with the word "endless." In stanza 12, it is entrance upon "endlesse matrimony"—marriage, which, in so many poems of the Renaissance (Shakespeare's sonnets, for instance) is a way of achieving eternal life through progeny. In stanza 24 it is the "endlesse moniment" which the poem is adjured to be: i.e., as many another Renaissance poem promises to be (others of Shakespeare's sonnets, and Spenser's, for instance), this one is an eternal, and eternizing, monument.

The reader may perhaps have noted in this catalogue that the correspondences, or pairings, seem to follow a certain system, which I have indicated by the arrangement of stanzas in the text at the end of this book. In each of the four cases so far outlined, a stanza from among the first twelve of the poem pairs with, or matches, the corresponding stanza among the second twelve, so as to give the series 9, 10, 11, 12 and 21, 22, 23, 24.

This scheme seems in fact to be followed also through the earlier parts of the two halves of the poem, so that, in total, stanzas 1–12 correspond in order to stanzas 13–24. Some of the pairings in the earlier parts of the series are, as before, more obvious than others. As might be expected in terms of such a scheme, Spenser refrains from appealing to the bride to awaken until stanza 5, for this stanza must correspond to stanza 17, in which night must arrive according to the measurement by stanza hours on the day of the wedding, as described in Chapter I. In stanza 5 he appeals to her to awaken; in stanza 17 he puts her to bed. There are stronger correspondences than this, however, in some of the stanzas from 5 (in the first series) and 17 (in the second) onwards, where Spenser is in a position to play on day and night. Thus stanza 7 contains a prayer to the sun to shine favorably, and not to burn the bride's face, and a prayer to Phoebus to let this one day be the poet's; the matching stanza 19 is a prayer to Night not to allow a number of grisly possibilities to come to pass. Also, in stanza 7 the poet promises to sing the praises of Phoebus, father of the Muse, for Spenser, putatively, has sung in such fashion as to delight this god; in stanza 19, on the other hand, the poet asks that none of a series of cacophonous noise-makers be allowed to "sing" "theyr drery accents." In another pair (8 and 20), stanza 8 is entirely given over to the noises of day: the minstrels "shrill"; their echoing music is heard from pipe, tabor, and fiddle; the damsels smite their timbrels; there is "carroling"; boys shout confusedly "Hymen, io Hymen," so that shouting fills the firmament. The people applaud and sing. Stanza 20, on the other hand, opens, "But let stil Silence trew night watches keep," and continues with the gentle nuptial activities of the quiet night. In addition the Alexandrian sons of Venus fluttering around the bed in this stanza seem to parallel the shouting boys running "up and downe the street," in stanza 8. This association by contrast of these two classes of beings is not foreign to Spenser's mind:

> A flocke of little loves, and sports, and joyes,
> With nimble wings of gold and purple hew;
> Whose shapes seem'd not like to terrestriall boyes,
> But like to Angels playing heavenly toyes . . .
>
> *(Faerie Queene* 4.10.42.2–5)

The matching stanzas from here to the end of the poem (9–12, 21–24) have already been described.

In the first four pairs of the series (before the bride is called to awaken in the first series, and before she is bedded in the second), Spenser cannot work with antitheses of, or parallels between, day and night, for this part of the poem is given over to day in both cases. Perhaps as a result of this, only two of the four sets of correspondences here are fairly plain. In stanza 1, the Muses, who have aided the poet to adorn others so that "even the greatest did not greatly scorne" to be thus honored, are now called upon by him to turn to the the praise of the poet's beloved in this poem itself. In the corresponding stanza 13 the angels, who are continually in the service of the Greatest around the sacred altar, aiding the priest, now forget their service and fly about the bride, peeping into her face; Spenser adjures them to sing "Alleluya." This parallelism between Muses and angels as singers of praise is certainly not an unfamiliar idea; moreover, Spenser uses it himself elsewhere, as when he speaks of Florimell's due in *Faerie Queene* 3.8.43 ("Fit song of Angels caroled to bee; / But yet what so my feeble Muse can frame . . ."), or as when speaking of the divine Sapience, whose beauty, unlike his bride's or Florimell's, is purely spiritual:

> Ah gentle Muse thou art too weake and faint,
> The pourtraict of so heavenly hew to paint.

> Let Angels which her goodly face behold
> And see at will, her soveraigne praises sing,
> And those most sacred mysteries unfold,
> Of that faire love of mightie heavens king.
>
> (*Hymne of Heavenly Beautie*, 230–35)

The pair of stanzas 3 and 15 involves an allusion of a different character. In 3 the Muses are told to gather together nymphs whose chief activity is to be flower gathering and garlanding. They are to come decked with garlands, with one for the bride; they are to make bridal posies and gather other flowers for the bridal chamber and for the bride to walk on. Furthermore, the muses themselves are to sing "this song" (i.e., *Epithalamion*). In the corresponding stanza 15 the day is indicated to be St. Barnabas', of which the chief popular activity in England is universally described, on very strong evidence, to have been garlanding with flowers.[2] Furthermore, the chief activity of the young townsmen addressed in this stanza is bell ringing: they are to ring the bells to make the day "weare away," which in one sense amounts to the same thing as the Muses of stanza 3 singing "this song," of which

[2] "Garlands of roses, of lavender, of rosemary, and of woodruff, were worn and were used for decorating the churches on St. Barnabas' day, as we find from old entries in church books" (quoted in A. R. Wright, *British Calendar Customs, England*, III [London, 1940], 1–2). Cf. entry for 1512 in John Brand, *Observations on Popular Antiquities*, with the additions of Sir Henry Ellis (London, 1877), art. "St. Barnabas' Day," p. 162; D. G. Spicer, *Yearbook of English Festivals* (New York, 1954), p. 81.

Another activity of the young men in stanza 15 is bonfire making. This, and bell ringing, may have been associated in local custom and in Spenser's mind with this day, but these activities are usually associated with Midsummer Eve, which, despite occasional modern statements to the contrary, was probably not St. Barnabas' Day (June 11) but St. John's Eve (June 23). Cf. *The Diary of Henry Machyn*, ed. J. G. Nichols (publications of the Camden Society, Vol. 42, 1848), p. 261 (under 1561): "The xxiij day of June, was Mydsomer-day, at Grenwyche was grett tryum(ph)." On account of the discrepancy between the Julian and Gregorian calendars, an Old St. Barnaby Day is now celebrated in some parts of England on June 22.

twenty-three stanzas, each presumably representing an hour, end with the word "ring." Perhaps to underline his intention, Spenser uniquely opens, as well as closes, this stanza with the same word.

Up to this point we have displayed the main evidence for pairing in nine of the twelve pairs of stanzas; three less obvious possibilities of pairing remain to be examined. In the nine already covered the question has been, not whether Spenser was successful in poetically embodying a pairing technique in *Epithalamion* (that cannot be decided until we know, at least, what his ultimate purpose was), but whether he had such an intention at all. As in the case of the numerical totals indicated in the preceding chapter, the evidence here emphatically makes it more reasonable to assume that he did than to suppose that he did not.

I have not considered here all the possibilities of parallels that I have been able to find in these eighteen stanzas, because demonstration is likely to be clogged by such details: I have reserved them for the glosses to the text at the end of this volume. The likelihood of pairing may be increased in stanzas 5 and 17, for example, by observing that the words "Why doe ye *sleepe* thus long,/ When meeter were that ye should now *awake*," of stanza 5 exhibit a parallelism to the situation of Maia when she is taken by Jove, "Twixt *sleepe* and *wake*, after she weary was," in stanza 17, or that the bird song, like that of a standard medieval spring opening connoting May (noticed by at least one other medievalist) [3] in stanza 5, may be parallel to the May goddess Maia of stanza 17. But of these two observations one involves no more than a probability, the other a slightly lesser degree of likelihood, and there is room for others of these only in the glosses. Undoubtedly I have missed some of the probabilities, and I may also have imputed a higher degree of convincingness to some others than is appropriate. The fact remains, however, that the main weight of the evidence

[3] C. S. Lewis, *English Literature in the Sixteenth Century* . . . (Oxford, 1954), p. 373.

in these nine pairs is considerable, as anyone may discover by at-
tempting (as the writer has done) to make combinations of these
stanzas on any other basis than 1–12 against 13–24.

The question with the three remaining possible pairs is of a
different nature: assuming, on the basis of evidence already presented, that Spenser had the intention here imputed to him, of
pairing stanzas 1–12 with stanzas 13–24, can any evidence be
found of this pairing in the three of the stanza pairs (2 and 14, 4
and 16, 6 and 18) that have not yet been examined? Such corrobo-
rative evidence is available, but it is mainly of a nature to elaborate
and complete the scheme of pairing, not to demonstrate it. Once
this evidence is accepted, it may contribute to a total impression of
Spenser's poetic success, but it is not, for the most part, likely to
convince anyone of Spenser's intention of pairing, unless he has
already been led towards conviction by the other nine pairs.

Stanza 4 (to take up first the clearest case) is an adjuration to
two classes of beings: water nymphs and maidens of the mountains.
The first of these are described in connection with fish: the nymphs
of the river Mulla, who tend its trout and pike (excelling all
others), and the nymphs of the lake where there are no fish. They
are all to bind up their locks, "the which hang scatterd light," and
to regard the reflection of their faces, "as the christall bright," in
the water. On the other hand, the maids of the heights are described as preserving the deer by chasing away the wolves with their
steel darts.

Stanza 16, which logically matches this stanza, is also concerned
with two objects: the planets Sol and Venus. The sun is adjured to
go down, and Venus appears in the east. She is the lamp of love,
with golden crest, who leads all the other heavenly bodies (because
she appears first in the evening sky, and because love rules all).
On the "glad many" celebrating the wedding feast she appears to
look down cheerfully from above, and to laugh "atweene her
twinkling light."

It seems to have been part of Spenser's intention here to match the fish-tending nymphs of stanza 4 with the planet Venus in stanza 16, since fish have associations with Venus. In Chaucer's *Squire's Tale,* which Spenser certainly knew well, since he continued it in *Faerie Queene* 4, we find this description of the amorous dancers and merrymakers at the banquet of Cambiuscan:

> Now dauncen lusty Venus children deere,
> For in the Fyssh hir lady sat ful hye,
> And looketh on hem with a freendly ye.
>
> *(Squire's Tale,* 272–74)

The situation here bears enough of a resemblance to that of the merrymakers of stanza 16 to make it possible that Spenser had this passage in mind, but the tradition which gave rise to it had a wide enough currency so that he could have happened on the idea elsewhere. The tradition is simply (as Skeat's note [4] to this passage makes clear) the astrological notion that the planet Venus was exalted in the sign of Pisces. Chaucer refers to it again in the *Wife of Bath's Prologue,* l. 704 ("In Pisces, wher Venus is exaltat"), and Sir Thomas Browne [5] says, "Who will not commend the wit of astrology? Venus, born out of the sea, hath her exaltation in Pisces." Spenser himself bears witness elsewhere to the association of Venus with fish:

> Therefore the antique wisards well invented,
> That *Venus* of the fomy sea was bred;
> For that the seas by her are most augmented.
> Witnesse th'exceeding fry, which there are fed,
> And wondrous sholes, which may of none be red.
>
> *(Faerie Queene* 4.12.2.1–5)

---

[4] *The Works of Geoffrey Chaucer,* ed. W. W. Skeat (Oxford, 1894), V, 381.

[5] Quoted by Skeat, *ibid.*

It is doubtful, however, that Spenser intends in stanza 16 to go beyond the mere association of Venus with fish, or of Venus with Pisces, to the actual location of the planet in that sign. It is true that when Dante misplaces Venus in *Purgatorio* 1.19–21, he does so in order to have her in Pisces.[6] It is also true, and most surprising, that Spenser misplaces Venus more drastically in stanza 16 by making her appear in the eastern sky (l. 287) as the sun nears the western horizon. This is an astronomical impossibility, as he almost surely must have known. She is seen near the sun—in the west at sundown, in the east at sunup: to this latter fact, at least, he bears witness at the beginning of an episode (the betrothal of Una and Redcross) which in its later stages, unquoted here, contains more verbal reminiscences of *Epithalamion* than any other in *The Faerie Queene*. He shows Una,

> . . . forth proceeding with sad sober cheare,
> As bright as doth the morning starre appeare
> Out of the East, with flaming lockes bedight,
> To tell that dawning day is drawing neare, . . .
>
> (1.12.21.4–7)

If then, as seems likely, he knew that Venus as the evening star always appears in the west, why does he put her in the east in the evening of *Epithalamion?* If he transferred her into the east on the assumption that he was putting her in Pisces, his lore was not very precise: this sign would have still been below the eastern horizon at the time when the sun in Cancer (l. 269) was nearing the western horizon. It is true that a calculation by an unlearned astronomer on the basis of assigning two hours of the twenty-four to each of the twelve zodiacal signs (a premise that can be held only

---

[6] The usual explanation for this is that he wished to follow the tradition as to the position of all the planets at the moment of creation, not to suggest her exaltation (see note to this passage in the Carlyle, Okey, Wicksteed edition of *La Divina Commedia*, London, 1933). I do not know whether the two ideas are associated.

for the time of the equinoxes) might have begun with Cancer on the eastern horizon at sunup, and would then have ended with Pisces in that position at sundown, sixteen and one quarter hours later. But we can base no conclusion on assumptions about Spenser's probable degree of imprecision (or bookishness), so that it seems best to adhere to the more neutral notion that he wished to express only a traditional association between Venus and fish. The sign on the eastern horizon in the given circumstances would actually have been Capricorn, but it is not part of our task here to reason about Venus' association with goats.

It may also be that Spenser has in mind a parallel between the nymphs asked to look at their reflections in the water in stanza 4, and Venus, leader of the heavenly host, looking down from above on the singing celebrators of the wedding in stanza 16. Since she leads the heavenly host, perhaps the conceit is that she sees a reflection of herself in the bride below, who influences the host of celebrators and inspires all who see her with love. The bride has been implicitly compared with Venus earlier in the poem, where she is given the goddess's regular attendants, the Hours and the Graces, which latter are to sing to her, "as ye use to Venus" (l. 108). Similarly, the golden crest, cheerful countenance, and "twinkling light" of the planet in stanza 16 may be cognate with the "christall bright" countenances and the locks, "the which hang scatterd light" of the nymphs in stanza 4, since the rays of a heavenly body are often compared, in classical and Renaissance poetry, to locks of hair (*e.g.*, in the passage about Una quoted above and in *Prothalamion*, ll. 164–65).

A connection between the two stanzas is thus shown to be possible, although it is not fully demonstrated. I find no quotation certainly known to Spenser which would link the other two classes of beings here—the mountain maidens who protect the deer against the wolf (in stanza 4), and the sun (in stanza 16), but it is quite likely that he would have known of that aspect of Apollo which protects various animals against the wolf.[7] The animals are usually sheep and cattle, but Apollo is also known as a protector of deer (a contamination from the Artemis cult is to be suspected).[8] Spenser may also have known of the allegorical interpretation according to which Apollo chasing away the wolf is said to be the sun dispelling winter or pestilence:[9] in stanza 4, the sun is presumably ascending (the maidens chase the wolves with their steel darts—perhaps the rays of the sun?); in stanza 16, the sun is in the opposite situation —about to descend beneath the horizon.

Stanzas 6 and 18 are the next pair to be considered. In stanza 6 the beloved is proclaimed to be awake: her eyes, previously like stars concealed by dark clouds, now show more brightly than Hesperus, the brightest evening star. The damsels are now to adorn her: first the Hours are to come, who were begotten of Day and Night in Jove's sweet paradise; they create and repair all worldly things that are fair. Then the Graces must help, and sing to her as they do to Venus. In stanza 18, on the other hand, Night (having arrived in stanza 17) is to spread her wing over the lovers and wrap them in her sable mantle, so that they will be invisible. Furthermore, Night is enjoined to see that this night is calm, like the one during which Jove begat Hercules on Alcmene, or like the one in which Jove begot Majesty on Night herself.

Here Spenser probably meant one parallel in this sense: as the Hours and Graces in stanza 6 are to adorn the bride with the

---

[7] The classical references to this are collected in Pauly-Wissowa, *Real-Encyclopädie der classischen Altertumswissenschaft*, art. "Apollon," and in Daremberg and Saglio, *Dictionnaire des antiquités*, art. "Apollo." Among works that Spenser is likely to have known, I find only, in Natalis Comes, that to Apollo, "lupus sacer existimatur, quia cum infestum sit animal gregibus et armentis, Apollonis tamen armento pepercerit." (I have used a late edition: *Mythologiae, sive explicationum fabularum . . . Parisiis, apud Arnoldum Sittart . . . , 1583, 3.16, p. 345.)

[8] Pauly-Wissowa, art. "Apollon," and Daremberg and Saglio, art. "Apollo."

[9] Daremberg and Saglio, art. "Apollo" (citing Sophocles, *Electra*, 6).

beauties of the day, so Night is to attire the bridal pair in her mantle and cover them with her wing. He also probably meant that,
as with the coming of day the eyes of the bride are like the evening star coming from behind a cloud into full visibility, so with
the coming of night the lovers retire into invisibility again beneath
the previously mentioned wing and mantle of Night. The most
interesting confrontation, however, involves, on the one side, the
procreation of the Hours by Day and Night in the garden of Jove
in stanza 6, and, on the other, the begetting of Majesty by Jove
on Night in stanza 18. In the Mutability Cantos, it is the Hours
who are begotten by Jove and Night (*Faerie Queene* 7.7.45.1–2),
of which the only explanation [10] is that the upper air, the day, and
light are aspects of Jove, so that in a sense the Hours of the Mutability Cantos are produced by Day and Night, as those of *Epithalamion* are. But, *mutatis mutandis,* the Hours of *Epithalamion*
probably appear to Spenser's syncretic imagination to be born of
Jove (since in one of his aspects he rules, or is, Day: *vide* the
Mutability Cantos) and of Night, in Jove's own sweet garden.
In that case, one product of Jove (i.e., Day) and Night—namely
the Hours—in stanza 6, is being paralleled with their other offspring—Majesty—in stanza 18. If this explanation appears
strained, so does Spenser's myth of Majesty born of Jove and
Night, for apparently he cut it out of whole cloth. It is not known
to have a precedent in any other author,[11] and Spenser's search
for a parallel to his myth of the birth of the Hours in stanza 6 may
be the explanation for his having invented it. All of this may also
be the key to the accompanying myth of Alcmene in stanza 18.
Perhaps she seemed appropriate to Spenser because in addition to
coupling with Jove (Day?) she also married Rhadamanthys, who,
belonging to the infernal regions, may represent night, when the
sun has gone beneath the earth. One may compare here Spenser's

[10] See Variorum note, VI, 308.
[11] See Variorum note, *Minor Poems*, II, 484.

classically motivated retirement of Night to Hell during the day
in *Faerie Queene* 1.5.31–44. Possibly, however, Spenser would
also have been influenced in his choice by the desire to suggest
that his marriage would produce offspring comparable to Alcmene's
son Hercules.

However speculative some of these points may seem concerning
stanzas 6 and 18, enough substance attaches to them to make
reasonable, if not to prove, Spenser's pairing of these two stanzas.

Stanzas 2 and 14 remain. Stanza 2 begins the action of the
marriage day (immediately after the invocation of the Muses in
stanza 1). Hymen is said to be awake and ready to set his Masque
into action, with its trim bachelors. The "wished day" of the wedding has come, which will pay a usury of long delight to the bride
for all the past pains and sorrows (three lines on the day). The
Muses are to sing of joy and solace. At the beginning of the stanza,
the point is made that the sun disperses the "unchearefull dampe"
of night. In stanza 14, "Now al is done." The action of the marriage proper is completed, and at the wine-swilling wedding feast
about to ensue, Hymen is to be crowned with wreaths, and so is
Bacchus. The joyfulness and holiness of the day are expatiated
on through four lines. The Graces are to dance, and the maidens
to sing their carol. The posts and walls are to be sprinkled with
wine so that they may sweat.

The possibilities of parallelism here are implicit in the way I
have enumerated some of the contents of these two stanzas: as the
action of the marriage may be said to begin in stanza 2, so it is
completed in stanza 14 (but it must be admitted that it may be
more logical to say that the action which begins in stanza 2 is that
of the whole poem, not simply of the marriage). The parallelism
in the appearance of Hymen in the two stanzas is more striking:
he is prayed to in stanza 22, but his only appearance as a part of
the action of the poem is in these two stanzas—2 and 14. The
discussion of the "day" itself in the two stanzas is also striking,

since no other passage of similar length on the day is to be found in the poem except in stanza 15, where it is a continuation of stanza 14, and where (as I hope to show later) a quite different symbolic purpose is in view. Finally, the singing Muses of stanza 2 may parallel the carolling maidens and dancing Graces of stanza 14, and the sun's dispersal of the nocturnal damp in stanza 2 may be played off against the re-creation of dampness by wetting the posts and walls with wine in stanza 14.

The parallels in stanzas 2 and 14 strike the present writer as the weakest of the lot in terms of proof (which says nothing about what they amount to poetically, once accepted), but they are sufficient to show the possibility of pairing in a context where pairing seems to be indicated. As already mentioned, Spenser is not in a position in this part of his poem to pair day symbols with night symbols, as he seems to have done later in the two series.

In the light of the foregoing, it would seem very probable that Spenser intended to pair the series 1–12 and 13–24 as indicated. Much could be said about the typically Spenserian allusiveness with which this is accomplished, so that objects seem to undulate and, losing their firm outlines, transform themselves into other things, as in *The Faerie Queene;* much needs to be thought and said before we shall have come to terms with the working of Spenser's imagination here. But it seems best at this point to restrict ourselves to the mere datum: Spenser seems to have paired these two series of stanzas.

But why did he do it? If a common denominator could be found for each of the two series, an explanation might soon be forthcoming; yet no quality seems to be common to either one. It was long ago noticed [12] that the poem reaches a climax in stanzas 12 and 13 (the marriage ceremony) but it seems impossible to conclude on the basis of this that Spenser intended the pairing feature in his poem to show a parallelism between its rising and falling actions,

[12] See Variorum note, *Minor Poems*, II, 647, SPENS.

since the pairing depends in many cases not upon the correlating of events of the marriage day, but upon symbolic equivalences, often mythological ones. Again, the divine (pagan and Christian both) and the celestial play a larger part in the second series than in the first, but their role in the second series is not exclusive (cf. the bell ringers of stanza 15), and they also intrude in the first series (cf., among many others, Phoebus in stanza 7).

Up to this point, then, we can make only a minimum assertion: Spenser has divided, and at the same time correlated, his stanzas in two different ways. By a system of pairing he has created the series 1–12 and 13–24. By a variation in refrains from positive to negative, he has separated his first sixteen stanzas from the following eight. Equally, he has correlated the series of both sets as well as separating them: each of the first twelve is logically related to the corresponding stanza of the second twelve; the variation from positive to negative in the refrains is only a variation in a fundamentally similar pattern.

We observe as well, on the basis of what has been shown in Chapter I, (1) that the twenty-four stanzas probably correspond in some fashion to the hours of the day, and (2) that the hours of light and of darkness on the wedding day—the longest day in the year—correspond to the division of the stanzas by refrains, and possibly to a further fractional division of stanza 17. We notice (3) that the total of long lines in the poem—365—suggests that Spenser is concerned in some fashion here with the days of the year as well as with the hours of the day—a contention supported by the attendance (unique in Spenser) of the Hours on the bride, in their significance as seasons of the year as well as hours of the day. We remind ourselves finally (4) that the long lines are divided as evenly as possible per stanza, except that the last stanza—the envoy—contains six, for reasons still to be explained, unless they prove inexplicable. What symbolic sense can ultimately be made of all this is the business of the next chapter.

III. ETERNITY IN MUTABILITY:
THE ENVOY

Looke how the Crowne, which *Ariadne* wore
Upon her yvory forehead that same day,
That Theseus her unto his bridale bore,
When the bold *Centaures* made that bloudy fray
With the fierce *Lapithes*, which did them dismay;
Being now placed in the firmament,
Through the bright heaven doth her beams display,
And is unto the starres an ornament,
Which round about her move in order excellent.
                                   (*Faerie Queene* 6.10.13)

If *Epithalamion* in one way embodies the year (as its 365 long
lines suggest), then one may legitimately wonder whether Spenser's
intention here is connected in some way with that in his other
noteworthy poetic celebration of the year, in the Mutability Cantos.
There, various divisions of the year (including Day and Night and
the Hours) and the personifications Life and Death march in
procession before Nature; her final decision after seeing them and
in the light of the other evidence provided by Dame Mutability is
that such cyclical change is not subject solely to mutability, but is
part of a universal, cyclical harmony by which all things return to
themselves, and, working their own perfection, remain, not simply
mutable, but (to borrow a phrase from *Faerie Queene* 3.6, where
the thought is parallel) "eterne in mutabilitie." It does not, of
course, follow that *Epithalamion*'s apparent embodiment of the year
is surely part of this particular nexus of Spenserian thinking. He
might have referred to the year in some entirely different context.
But it is certainly possible that this particular symbolic reference

to the year mirrors the preoccupation of the symbolism in the Mutability Cantos, and that Spenser wishes in this marriage ode, as he did in that work, to give symbolic expression to that Boethian-Chaucerian consolation by which man is seen to mirror the larger scheme of nature in continually re-creating and regenerating himself according to the harmony of the natural plan.

We can approach this feature of the present theory of interpretation only after a detailed investigation, which will expose the other main feature of the theory: this is that the two sets of circumstances set forth in the last two paragraphs of the preceding chapter are meant by Spenser to be complementary, and that they play, so to speak, into each other's hands.

1. The first of these two sets has to do with the two divisions (and correlations) created among the twenty-four stanzas, which in some fashion represent hours and are associated with the personified Hours who attend the bride: these stanzas form two matching series, twelve and twelve; and they are divided in a second way—by the division between light and darkness and by the change of refrain—into one group of sixteen and a fraction and into another of seven and a fraction. One way of investigating what Spenser intended by these divisions is to establish precisely his conception of the Hours in certain of his other works. It may then be easier to see what symbolic purpose his stanzas fulfill here, insofar as they represent hours.

He of course knew the twenty-four hours of the solar day in common usage, and he was acquainted with the Hours in one of their classical significances as seasons of the year; but it can be shown that in his most important use of the hours in his other works he depends upon another traditional conception of them.[1] This conception, found in classical and later authors, is the familiar one of the sidereal hours in modern astronomy.

[1] See Appendix for descriptions and documentation of traditions of the Hours.

The Hours of the procession in the Mutability Cantos, as daughters of Jove (Day) and Night, are porters

> Of heavens gate (whence all the gods issued)
> Which they did dayly watch, and nightly wake
> By even turnes. . . .
>
> *(Faerie Queene* 7.7.45)

That is to say, they are stationed in the sky, according to a traditional notion, to superintend the rising above the horizon (the word gives us the Greek root to which "hour" and "horoscope" are related) of the various heavenly bodies, named after the figures of the classical pantheon. Each of these rises in turn in the orient (here the Latin root is used to which "hour" is related) and pursues its way across the sky, to sink in the occident; and this goes on day and night, although during the day the light of the sun generally hides the other heavenly bodies from our sight. These Hours —twenty-four of them—must be imagined as stationed at equal distances from each other, from east to west, all the way around the heavenly sphere, in accordance with modern astronomical habit. That Spenser so imagined them appears from a passage in *An Hymne of Heavenly Love:*

> Ere flitting Time could wag his eyas wings
> About that mightie bound, which doth embrace
> The rolling spheres, and parts their houres by Space. . . .
>
> (24–26)

The "spheres" are of course the Ptolemaic ones—the sphere of the fixed stars, revolving about the earth once daily, and the other spheres of the planets arranged concentrically within the starry sphere and also revolving with it, although they have other motions of their own as well. The Hours are thought of as defining the relationship between space and time in the heavens: at fixed distances around the outermost bounds of the moving heavens are stationed Hours; these, dividing the heavens along lines (now called "hour-circles") running in a north-south direction from one heavenly pole to another, divide up the firmament so that to every heavenly body is assigned its appropriate Hour for rising, and for setting as well. They are always thought of as revolving with the heavens: Milton, for instance, so recognizes them in his "circling Hours" (*Paradise Lost*, 6.3; *Paradise Regained*, 1.57), and although Spenser does not define their motion in this passage, the fact that he imagines them as moving with the heavens follows from something else—of great importance here—which is contained in the passage quoted from the Mutability Cantos.

There we are told that the Hours watch the gates of heaven (i.e., the horizon) daily and nightly "by even turnes." It follows from this, in the first place, that the Hours move with the heavens, since some of them must arrive at the horizon by day and others by night; they are not fixed in the heavens while the heavenly bodies move past them, for then only one hour would supervise the rising of all the heavenly bodies. A second deduction, however, follows from the statement that the Hours take turns in the matter of daily and nightly duties. Certainly Spenser does not mean simply that one fixed company of Hours always fulfills the duties of the night and another one, in turn, always fulfills those of the day, for then the turns would almost never be even: only at the two equinoxes are the number of hours of light equal to those of darkness. He means, rather, an interchange of duties by which, during the course of the year, the sidereal Hours are continually shifting in their relation to the sun, which of course controls day and night. This qualification, in fact, is what shows that Spenser follows in detail the most important of the traditional conceptions of the personified Hours of the day, the one that survives in modern astronomical practice. If the Hours are stationed around the outer bounds of the revolving spheres, as the passage from *An Hymne of Heavenly Love* suggests, then they are stationed in or on the sphere of the fixed stars, the outermost visible one (or—what amounts to essentially the same thing here—in or on the additional sphere enclosing and moving all the others, the fixed stars included); and if they revolve with the sphere of the fixed stars, then they must in fact take turns in the execution of daily and nightly duties, in accordance with a peculiar feature of the relationship between the motion of the planet Sol and that of the fixed stars. This feature is most easily described in Ptolemaic terms, as Spenser himself imagined it, but its essential character has been known since time immemorial.

Roughly speaking, all the spheres—that of the fixed stars as well as those of the planets contained concentrically within it—revolve once from east to west every day, but this statement is only approximate: the planets hang back a little daily, because their motion is minutely slower than that of the fixed stars. Thus, when the starry sphere has completed a full revolution of 360° around the earth, in slightly less than twenty-four solar hours, the sun, for instance, will have completed only about 359°; it hangs back daily about one degree, and has changed its position slightly in relation to the fixed stars above it. This circumstance of the sun's movement is alluded to in *Epithalamion*: ". . . declining daily by degrees,/ He somewhat loseth of his heat and light,/ When once the Crab behind his back he sees" (ll. 267–69). Hanging back thus daily the sun follows a line which can be plotted from west to east among the fixed stars forming its background. This line is the ecliptic, running along the center of the starry path called the zodiac. As the sun drops back daily, it finally makes a complete eastward circle of the starry firmament along this path and returns in 365 days to its original place, giving us our definition of the year: that is to say, dropping back daily $\frac{1}{365}$ of a circle—very nearly one degree—it must complete its own west to east circle in the time we all know.

It is plain that the sun must also drop back against the background of the hours, just as it does against that of the fixed stars, if the hours are conceived of as stationed equidistantly in an east-west circle around the starry sphere. Every fifteen or sixteen days the sun, retarded $\frac{1}{365}$ of a circle daily as compared with the starry firmament, will pass over from the realm of one hour, across a dividing line called by modern astronomers an hour-circle, into the realm of another hour, which encompasses $15°$ or $\frac{1}{24}$ of a circle. The sun will then rise and set in that hour, as it had previously risen and set in the one to the west of it. In the course of 365 days, the sun will have occupied, and risen and set in, the space of each of the hours in turn, returning finally to the one from which it started.

One further deduction from these circumstances will take us back to Spenser's Hours: just as the hour in which the sun rises and sets is constantly changing, so are the hours which rise above the horizon in turn during the period of daylight, and those which rise at night. Each of these two series of hours is constantly being augmented at one end and decreased at the other, as the sun rises and sets constantly in an hour further to the east. The practical result of this, since these hours are simply spatial indications on the starry firmament, is that the sky and the heavenly bodies which the hours, so to speak, shepherd above the horizon during the night are slowly and constantly being exchanged against the opposite portion of the firmament superintended by the hours of day. At the beginning and end of any period of twelve months, the portion of the sky exposed at night will be the same, and so will the portion exposed in daylight. But at the beginning and end of just half that time—six months—the position of the day and night skies, and of the hours, will be reversed in relation to the sun, which has completed only half its annual journey. As Caxton puts it: [2]

But the sterres that ben over us in the somer on the day tyme, in wynter they be over us in the nyght; and they that be under us in the wynter be over us in the somer; ffor the sonne that goth round aboute us taketh fro tho sterres their clernes that ben on the day tyme where the sonne is, unto the tyme that he draweth hym under.

Now this constant interchange between the stellar (i.e., sidereal) hours of day and those of night is apparently the only explanation for Spenser's words about the Hours in the Mutability Cantos: they daily watch and nightly wake by even turns, because, according to the positions of the sun in its annual journey, they are constantly exchanging day and night duties. We thus conclude that Spenser here imagines the hours for poetic purposes according to the tradition which has survived in modern astronomy: for him, as for some of his predecessors (see the Appendix), and for Milton, and in the usage of the modern astronomer, they are sidereal hours, dividing the firmament into twenty-four regions, each extending from one celestial pole to the other; furthermore they revolve with the apparent revolution of the fixed stars and move in any period of six months to opposite positions in the celestial sphere when measured against the sun's measure of day and night.

Having come to as precise a notion of Spenser's conception of the Hours as we can in his most important hitherto known use of them we now return to *Epithalamion:* the only workable interpretation which the present author has been able to discover for the pairing of stanzas 1–12 with stanzas 13–24 in this poem depends on the assumption that Spenser conceives of the Hours of day and night here as he does in the passage from the Mutability

[2] *Caxton's Mirrour of the World,* ed. O. H. Prior, EETS, Ex. Ser. CX (1913 for 1912), pp. 133–34.

Cantos, and in the lines from *An Hymne of Heavenly Beautie*. This interpretation must now be outlined.

We have already shown why it seems necessary to believe that the poem in one way represents the passage of a year, and how it is possible to suppose that the seasons of the year are in some fashion connected with Spenser's symbolic intention, since the Hours who are attendants on the bride are not simply daily ones, but also "allot" these seasons, like the classical Horae. My interpretation is, briefly, that the divisions, and collations, of the stanzas (which apparently represent the twenty-four hours) symbolize the situations of the daily sidereal hours at the four seasons of the year. We can perceive the feasibility of this theory by attending to three features of the poem: (1) the divisions between day and night on the day of the marriage, (2) the pairing itself, and (3) the fact that this pairing splits the poem in half at its midway point.

At the most obvious symbolic level we have been able to show, the poem represents the situation of the hours at the summer solstice: at that time, the longest day in the year, the sun has been moving not only eastward, but also upward (i.e., northward) in the sky, for the axis of the sun's annual eastward circle is askew to that of the daily westward revolution, so that the sun is always verging either north or south of its generally eastward annual course, depending on the time of year. At this date, in executing its movement toward the northeast quarter, along the path of the zodiac and into the sign of the Crab, the sun has reached its northernmost annual point, after which (as Spenser says in stanza 15) its generally eastward course will incline towards the south. But at this point in the calendar, at its highest point in the sky for the northern hemisphere, its daily journey from east to west will be above the horizon for a longer period of time than on any other day in the year—sixteen and a fraction hours, as we know, in the latitude of Spenser's marriage; and it will be below the hori-

zon for only seven and a fraction hours. All of this seems to be
symbolized by the division in the poem between the positive and
negative refrains and by the coming of night in the seventeenth
stanza. Approximately the same situation holds if the stanzas are
regarded as sidereal hours: that is, the same kind of hours, circling
around the starry firmament, that Spenser seems to mean in the
Mutability Cantos; from dawn, when the sun's disc touches the
eastern horizon in its appropriate hour, sixteen and a fraction hours
will rise above the eastern horizon, bringing their appropriate
heavenly bodies with them, until the sun's disc touches the western
horizon; and seven and a fraction hours will emerge during the
course of the night.

But in addition to symbolizing the hours of day and night at
the summer solstice by the device of positive and negative refrains,
Spenser has done something else, as we know: he has paired each
of his stanzas with another one twelve stanzas away from it
(backwards or forwards), or, to put it another way, he has suggested some kind of equivalence between any one stanza and another stanza separated from it by half the length of the poem;
and this feature is equivalent to the situation of the sidereal hours
in one important respect: any one of these twenty-four hours is
precisely opposite, in the celestial sphere, another hour which is
twelve hours, or one hemisphere, away from it, and the first of
these exchanges its position with the other, in regard to day and
night, in precisely half a year. Furthermore, in matching his
stanzas against each other, Spenser has chosen to end one series
at the end of stanza 12 and the other at the end of stanza 24 (he
could, for instance, have made one series stanzas 7 through 18,
and the other series stanzas 19–24, 1–6, conceiving the poem as a
circle, with its tail in its mouth). Splitting the poem thus, he has
in effect given us a counterpart of the situation of the sidereal hours
at the equinoxes of both spring and autumn: that is to say, on the
analogy of the other and more apparent division by stanzas be-

tween night and day, the first twelve hours (i.e., stanzas) represent those of day at the vernal equinox; the second twelve those of night, but by the poetic device of equivalence or interchangeability, the first twelve stanzas also represent the situation at the equinox of autumn, for at that time the sidereal hours have exchanged position: the former day hours are now night hours, and vice versa, because the celestial hemispheres now stand in an opposite relation to the sun. Furthermore, just as the split between day and night at the literal level of the poem gives us the analogy for supposing that the other division between the stanzas has to do with the division between light and darkness, so this further step in the symbolism yields a further analogy by which Spenser symbolically expresses the situation of the winter solstice: at the summer solstice the day hours are identified by their positive refrains, the night hours by negative ones, but on the same system of interchangeability as with the equinoxes, the series of seven and a fraction stanzas set off from the others by negative refrains and the arrival of night represent the hours of day, which, as Donne conveniently reminds us in the *Nocturnal upon St. Lucy's Day*, are seven and a fraction; and the sixteen stanzas with positive refrains represent the hours of the longest night in the year, when, as before, the celestial hemispheres reverse the relationship to the sun at the summer solstice.

To sum up, then: we have shown what Spenser's conception of the hours seems to have been in two of his other works; assuming his conception of them to have been the same in *Epithalamion*, a coherent interpretation of the device of the paired stanzas can be built on the theory that Spenser's symbolic intent here was to indicate the positions of the heavens in relation to the sun at the four seasons of the year, and the lengths of day and night at the four climactic points of the sun's annual progress. A connection with the Hours "Which doe the seasons of the yeare allot" (l.

100) is thus to be suspected, and with the allusions to the longest and shortest days and nights in stanza 15.

There is a certain elegance to the system just described which lends a degree of plausibility to it as mirroring Spenser's intention. Furthermore, it is extremely difficult, in the context of what has been shown so far, to discover any other possible interpretation of the facts.[3] Nevertheless, what has just been suggested is very far from our previous notion of the pattern of this remarkable poem, and it is at first sight very complicated; it will not be surprising, consequently, if some readers will find it difficult to believe that Spenser could really have meant all this. But a further set of circumstances at the end of the poem provides a corroboration of the theory and a further development of *Epithalamion*'s symbolism in a very solid and self-contained way. These matters bring us, as well, to the enormously affecting symbol of the human condition—of our tragic insufficiency inextricably interwoven with our compensation—which I believe Spenser has built into his poem.

2. Two apparently curious circumstances are germane here. One, the length and rime scheme of the envoy, has already been

[3] Only one other conceivable explanation has occurred to me. This depends on the tradition of the "unequal hours," as used, for instance, by Chaucer (Cf. Robinson's note to *Knight's Tale*, ll. 2217, 2271, in his editions of *The Works of Geoffrey Chaucer*, 1933, 1957). According to this the period between sunrise and sunset is divided into twelve units called hours, and so with the "hours" of night; these hours are equal in length to the usual ones only at the equinoxes. Spenser might thus be symbolizing the division between light and darkness on the day of his marriage by the 16-8 division of stanzas for our usual, "equal" hours, and by the 12-12 division of the "unequal" hours. But why would he have done this? He does not allude elsewhere to the unequal hours, and more than one division of his marriage day seems superfluous. Furthermore, this explanation offers no help in the matter of the equivalences between stanzas, or that of the 365 days of the year. The explanation which is given in the text, however, does so, and is directly complementary to the points made in the next division of this chapter.

alluded to: it is difficult to understand how Spenser settled on six long lines and one short one for this stanza, for it is like nothing else he did, and it is not written in a rime scheme familiar in Renaissance or medieval poetry. The other circumstance is the number of long lines per stanza. As previously indicated, each of the first twenty-three stanzas contains either fifteen or sixteen long lines, which is the most even division possible on the premise that Spenser wished his poem to contain just 365 long lines. As we may now suspect, he may have had another purpose in mind here: on its annual journey around the celestial sphere, the sun passes through the region of each of the twenty-four celestial hours in a period of between fifteen and sixteen days, moving $\frac{1}{365}$ of a circle daily. It would thus be satisfactory to symbolize this phenomenon approximately by assigning to some stanzas fifteen, to other sixteen long lines, so as to reach the total of 365 at the end of the poem. If he had done this with ideal symmetry, he would have ended *Epithalamion* with a stanza much like the last one in *Prothalamion,* which follows the metrical scheme of the other stanzas of the poem and is not an envoy. But this he did not do in *Epithalamion,* for he has assigned sixteen instead of fifteen long lines to so many of his stanzas that by the end of stanza 23 he is nine long lines ahead of himself, and has only six left over for the envoy, to complete the tale of 365. Why did he do this, instead of taking advantage of a possibility for symbolic symmetry that he must have been acquainted with? On any reckoning, the most even division of long lines among the twenty-four stanzas would seem appropriate, if (as it now seems necessary to believe) they represent in one sense hours of the day.

The only possible explanation for the curious formal character of the envoy and for the apparently conscious avoidance of an apparently desirable symmetry seems to be that Spenser had in mind yet another symbolic purpose, which actually finds expression closer to the surface meaning of the poem than the device which has already been described: he wished to indicate that circumstance of the sun's daily journey from east to west upon which its annual journey from west to east depends, and upon which, consequently, depend the seasons and the differences between the lengths of day and night as well. According to this interpretation, the long lines represent not simply days of the year and (approximately) degrees (i.e., $\frac{1}{365}$'s) of the sun's annual movement, but also degrees of the sun's *daily* movement, from east to west, along with the other heavenly bodies. In registering this movement, Spenser would of course be closer to the literal meaning of his poem, which is after all the record of a day's happenings, than he was in indicating the 365 annual steps through which the sun progresses. The interpretation about to be offered in these terms has several advantages: it explains in the first place the disparities noted above, and it also shows Spenser complementing the already explicated symbolism of the year and of the seasonal points of the sun's movement with a further symbolic device which signifies the related feature of the sun's diurnal movement, so that *Epithalamion* becomes in one sense a small working model of the total behavior of man's temporal source of light and life. In addition, this interpretation entails a satisfactory, if only partial, explanation of Spenser's meaning in one of his obscurest passages: the envoy itself. The insufficiency and imperfection in the sun's daily movement as compared with the movement of the fixed stars becomes the point of the symbolism, for this insufficiency has as its other face the creation of the cycle of the year and the seasons, just as our mortality is but one aspect of our lot, the other being cyclical regeneration and birth—the ultimate point of a marriage ode.

The relationship between the sun's daily apparent orbit around the earth and the similar movement of the starry sphere and of the sidereal hours has already been explained: during the period when the hours and the sphere of the fixed stars move through a

complete circle of 360°, the sun moves through only 359°: it
hangs back one degree, as Spenser mentions in the poem, because
its annual movement in the opposite direction slows it down
minutely. In a sense it is upon this daily hanging back that the
year, with all the variety of its seasons and the whole rhythm of
organic life, depends, for without it the sun could not forge along
its rising and falling eastward path of the zodiac. Yet this falling
short is, in some logical sense, an imperfection. In the traditional
understanding of this matter, the sun, as a planet, has two movements, and is errant and imperfect when compared with the
starry heaven in the perfect consistency of its single movement.
The thought that the stars possess a greater perfection than the
planets, and are nearer to the final perfection of Eternity, is a
common one, going back as far as the *Timaeus;* Spenser alludes
to the idea, in any case, in *Faerie Queene* 7.2.55.

Now, long line 359 of *Epithalamion* is the last line of stanza
23; it is my contention here that through the meaning, as well
as the length, of the envoy, Spenser wishes to communicate the
relationship between the daily shortcomings of the sun and the
total measure of 365 days created by this shortcoming, and between the 359 long lines of the full-size stanzas and the 365 long
lines of the poem complete with envoy. The contention must be
supported by considerable study of this last stanza, which is perhaps the most obscure passage in all of Spenser's works.

In the first place, the most accurate term to describe it is
probably *tornata,* and not "envoy," which is a word of more general import. The character of this last stanza gives us our best
reason for thinking that Spenser wished to give to *Epithalamion*
the form of a *canzone,* that is to say, a fairly long lyric containing
stanzas of indeterminate lengths and ending typically with a short
stanzaic address, called a *tornata,* to the completed poem. This
address in its first line typically calls upon the poem itself, with
the word *canzone* or "song," as though it were complete without

the *tornata*, and often goes on to assign the poem some duty. Petrarch, for instance, in his *canzone Sì è debile il filo a cui s'attene*, ends with a short stanza pathetically directing his song to prostrate itself before his lady and tell her that he will return to her when he can:

> Canzon, s'al dolce loco
> La donna nostra vedi,
> Credo ben che tu credi
> Ch'ella ti porgerá la bella mano,
> Ond'io son sí lontano.
> Non la toccar; ma reverente ai piedi
> Le di' ch'io sarò lá tosto ch'io possa,
> O spirto ignudo od uom di carne e d'ossa.

Spenser himself apparently translated [4] a version by Clément Marot of Petrarch's *canzone Standomi un giorno*, producing the following *tornata*:

> My Song thus now in thy Conclusions,
> Say boldly that these same six visions
> Do yelde unto thy lorde a sweete request,
> Ere it be long within the earth to rest.

$$(77-80)$$

All the characteristics given here for a *canzone* hold for *Epithalamion*, as has long been recognized. It is likely that Spenser chose this form because it allowed him to do in a traditional way what he wished to do: he could vary the length of his stanzas and make use of his envoy in a particular way, without doing something unprecedented. Certainly he has left us no other *canzone* in this strict sense, except for his youthful translation, and the form is rare in English, in his time or any other. Equally, of course,

---

[4] "Epigrams," in *A Theatre for Worldlings* (*Works of Edmund Spenser. A Variorum Edition*, VIII, 5–11).

it may have occurred to him first to try writing a *canzone* (the form as an epithalamium is not unprecedented on the Continent),[5] and the scheme of the year and the day as here outlined may have occurred to him later; or he may have been following some as yet undiscovered model for this scheme. Of these things we cannot be sure, but what seems to have served him well in his symbolic schemes at the end of the poem is the particular role which the *tornata* traditionally performs: it is both outside and inside the poem. Ostensibly, it is an address—a separate statement—to an already complete poem, at which it looks back. In fact, however, it always forms part of the poem and of the total poetic effect. In *Epithalamion* the seeming separation between the *tornata* and the rest of the poem is fairly drastic: the closing three lines of stanza 23 seem to conclude the poem then the *tornata* resumes, in a quite different and mystifying tone. The interpretation offered here (to repeat) is that Spenser ostensibly ends his poem in its 359th long line, symbolizing in one way the incomplete circle of the sun at the time when the heavenly hours and the celestial sphere are completing theirs, but that the envoy, adding six more long lines, expresses symbolically what this daily incompleteness of the sun entails: the creation of the measure of the solar years of 365 days, symbolized by the 365 long lines of the poem including its *tornata*. On this assumption, the symbolism at the end of the poem complements the symbolic indications of the year, of its four seasonal points, and of the lengths of night and day at these points, for it and they are created by the approximate one degree daily retrograde movement of the sun, as we have already shown.

The intention which I impute to him involves him in an apparent inconsistency: this is that the 359 lines representing the 359° movement of the sun in one sidereal day should be spread

[5] Cf. such a one by Marino, ending in a *tornata:* "Urania. Epitalamio nelle Nozze degl' Illustriss. Sig. Gio. Vincenzo Imperiali, & Caterina Grimaldi," in *Li epitalami del Cav. Marino* (Venice, 1664), pp. 114–16.

over twenty-four stanzas, not twenty-three, if these stanzas are
to represent hours. He apparently cannot escape from this inconsistency if he wishes to represent at the same time the annual movement of the sun through all the sidereal hours in 365 days. Yet
the inconsistency is only an apparent one, if the sidereal hours are
to be taken as representing degrees of space on the celestial sphere,
and not simply measures of time, for the sun actually moves
diurnally *with* its own sidereal hour for the day (at a minutely
slower rate of speed); it is only the annual movement that traces
a path against the background of the celestial hours. Consequently, any symbolism in the poem of the sun's daily movement
in degrees is, strictly speaking, independent of the scheme by which
the sun is shown moving annually from the realm of one hour
into that of another. Yet even from this solely apparent inconsistency Spenser escapes wittily in terms of what he says in the
tornata, to the meaning of which we now turn our attention.

> Song made in lieu of many ornaments,
> With which my love should duly have bene dect,
> Which cutting off through hasty accidents,
> Ye would not stay your dew time to expect,
> But promist both to recompens,
> Be unto her a goodly ornament,
> And for short time an endlesse moniment.

The first point that we may notice about these lines is that, in
matching this stanza with stanza 12, Spenser depended most obviously upon the words "due," "duly," and "endless," which appear nowhere in the poem outside these two stanzas. In stanza
12 "honour *dew*" to the bride consists in adornment of the temple; in stanza 24, the song is "made in lieu of many ornaments,"
with which the bride should "*duly* have bene dect," and the song
is reproached for not arriving at its "*dew* time." The criterion

of "due"-ness, or suitability, is thus applied to two concepts—
ornaments and time—and on both scores the song is regarded as
deficient. However, the concepts ornament and time reappear in
the last two lines; here the song is adjured to be a "goodly" (i.e.,
at least satisfactory or suitable) ornament, and (using the other
word from stanza 12) an "endlesse" monument for "short
time." A parallelism seems to be established between the first
appearance of the concepts ornament and time in the first four
lines, and their second appearance in the last two lines; but in the
first case the song is deprecated for falling short on both counts;
while in the second it is paradoxically viewed as capable of being
"goodly" as an ornament and "endlesse" (i.e., eternal) in the
matter of time.

It is because of both the parallelism and the paradox that it
seems proper to interpret the word "both" in the fifth line of this
stanza, between the two appearances of the concepts ornament
and time, as applying to these two concepts in their first appearance; that is (to paraphrase), both for the shortcoming of the
song as a due ornament and for its failure to arrive at its due
time, the song itself has been paradoxically promised in order to
recompense, or make up for, its own two deficiencies, so that it is
told to be (1) a goodly ornament (instead of being a mere substitute for the ornaments *due* the bride) and (2) an eternal monument to time (in place of having missed its *due* time).

Having established the possibility of this fundamental syntactical
pattern, we turn now to what Spenser is likely to have meant
specifically by the clause "Ye would not stay your dew time to
expect." The only other instances of Spenser's use of the expression "due time" (*Faerie Queene* 1.7.9.6, and 6.12.6.5) are in
connection with birth: [6] the "due time" of birth after complete

---

[6] I am indebted to Professor William Nelson for pointing this out to me.
See C. G. Osgood, *A Concordance to the Poems of Edmund Spenser* (Washington, 1915), "due."

gestation. If he has used the expression in this sense here, he is saying to his song, "You would not stay to await your due time for coming forth as a complete poem, but were born before you were fully formed." But the passage may also be interpreted with a more neutral meaning for "due time," and without the suggestion that the poem was imperfect when it came forth. The line would then mean simply, "You would not stay to await your due time, but arrived before that time." Both these interpretations, however, raise a problem: it is easy enough, on the one hand, to understand how *Epithalamion* could, as a "goodly ornament," form a recompense for the other ornaments (whatever they were) that were due the bride; but in the matter under review, what are we to make of the combined notions (1) that it is a blemish upon a literary composition to reach completion before the time at which it is due, and (2) that its being an eternal monument to short time is specifically a recompense for its arriving before its due time? If Spenser had meant that *Epithalamion* was too hastily written to be satisfactory, he could hardly call it an eternal monument. On the other hand, if he meant that it arrived before its due time in any other sense than not being fully born and complete, we cannot imagine why this would have constituted an imperfection for which a recompense was needed.

From this apparent logical impasse there seems to be one principal means of escape: the song is incomplete and born before its due time at the end of its twenty-third stanza, before its *tornata,* having accreted only 359 long lines, just as the orbit of the sun in incomplete, having amounted to only 359°, at the time when the starry sphere has closed its circle; yet this symbolic insufficiency of the song celebrating a day contains the promise of a recompense in and through the *tornata* which the ostensible insufficiency of the song itself calls forth, just as the daily insufficiency of the sun contains the promise of the year—the main extrahuman expression of that sufficient and perfect cyclical order by which, as Spenser has it in the Mutability Cantos, we, and the whole universe of time and space, exist through Short Time. The first twenty-three stanzas of the song are thus properly described as arriving incomplete, as being born before their "due time"; and the sun similarly does not "stay" to await its "dew time," for, embarked on another journey, it will not stand fixed with the stars in their sphere to be carried around the circle in their due time of a sidereal day.

Two attitudes towards the temporal order are distinguishable in the Mutability Cantos, and both of these are touched on in stanzas 22, 23, and 24 of *Epithalamion*. The first of these is affirmative. The procession of the year and of life and death, and all the other evidences which Mutability produces to confirm her sway in the universe, elicit from Nature the statement that change is only one part of the process; things return to themselves again in an ordered dance:

> I well consider all that ye have sayd,
> And find that all things stedfastnes doe hate
> And changed be: yet being rightly wayd
> They are not changed from their first estate;
> But by their change their being doe dilate:
> And turning to themselves at length againe,
> Doe work their owne perfection so by fate:
> Then over them Change doth not rule and raigne;
> But they raigne over change, and doe their states maintaine.
>
> (*Faerie Queene* 7.7.58)

Evidently her dictum applies (1) to mortal life, which is symbolized in the procession by the figures Life and Death (7.7.46); (2) to the year, of which the divisions form the preceding part of the procession (7.7.28–45); and (3) to the sun, which is symbolized in the procession (7.7.44.9), but more importantly is

condemned by Mutability, along with the other planets, for having more than a single, simple motion—mainly, that is, for being
caught up in the annual as well as the daily journies which we have
described for the sun itself, although each of the other planets also
has an annual journey of its own:

> Besides, the sundry motions of your Spheares,
> So sundry waies and fashions as clerkes faine,
> Some in short space, and some in longer yeares;
> What is the same but alteration plaine?
>
> (*Faerie Queene* 7.7.55.1–4)

In a sense, the whole of *Epithalamion* as a marriage ode and a
register of time expresses the paradox of this first, affirmative attitude—that in spite of the subjection of life to change and death,
and in spite of the subjection to mutability of the most important
of the heavenly bodies, nevertheless the individual, mortal life of
man is renewed in generation, just as the insufficiency of the sun
is recompensed in its annual journey, with all the recurring, time-
given variety so created. But all of this is touched on more explicitly in the last three stanzas than elsewhere in the poem. The
appeal for progeny to inherit the earth in stanzas 22 and 23 bears
witness to the traditional estimate of "endlesse matrimony" as the
institution through which life is reasserted over the forces of
death, just as life is described as doing in the Garden of Adonis
of *Faerie Queene* 3.6; and in the last stanza the course of the
sun on the day of the marriage is allegorically (or "darkly," as
Spenser might have said) described as incomplete, but achieving
a completeness and perfection of another kind.

In addition to this paradoxical affirmation of the mortal life of
man and the world of time and space, another attitude, similarly
traditional, closes both the Mutability Cantos and *Epithalamion*.
Turning at the end of the Cantos from the celebration of an

eternity in mutability to the acknowledgment of a greater Eternity, Spenser takes in hand the theme *De contemptu mundi.* In all things below, change seems to bear the greater sway,

> Which makes me loath this state of life so tickle
> And love of things so vaine to cast away;
> Whose flowring pride, so fading and so fickle,
> Short *Time* shall soon cut down with his consuming sickle.

It would be indecorous in a marriage ode to suggest a disharmony in this way between the heavenly and the earthly, but there is certainly a hint of the same disparagement in one of the meanings of the epithet "short time" in the concluding line of *Epithalamion.* More importantly, the affirmation of the stasis—the "rest"—of all things upon the pillars of Eternity, when we have left the realm of time, as described in the last lines of *The Faerie Queene,*

> For all that moveth, doth in *Change* delight:
> But thence-forth all shall rest eternally
> With him that is the God of Sabbaoth hight:
> O! that great Sabbaoth God, grant me that Sabaoths sight,

is mirrored in the *requiescamus in spe* of stanza 23 of *Epithalamion,* concluding the appeal that the wedded pair's posterity may, after long and happy lives, take their places as saints in heavenly tabernacles:

> So let us rest, sweet love, in hope of this,
> And cease till then our tymely joyes to sing,
> The woods no more us answer, nor our eccho ring.

The catholicity with which Spenser can turn from the celebration of life and short time, both in the Cantos and in his marriage ode, to the celebration of eternity is the same Boethian catholicity with which Chaucer's Theseus turns from expressing satisfaction that Arcite has left the "foule prisoun of this lyf" (*Knight's Tale,*

3061), to compassing the marriage in this world of Emily and Palamon, partly for a reason which he has already given us: ". . . speces of thynges and progressiouns/ Shullen enduren by successiouns,/ And nat eterne . . ." (3013–15). It is even more noteworthy that in Spenser's model for the judgment of Nature in the Cantos—that is to say, *The Parlement of Foules*—Chaucer turns with similar catholicity from affirming, at the beginning of his poem, the pettiness of the earth in the light of eternity (50–70), to celebrating at its end the theme of marriage and generation under the governance of Nature. Seen in this light, *Epithalamion* forms one more feature in the image of the Boethian-Chaucerian Spenser which C. S. Lewis [7] and J. A. W. Bennett [8] have given us, and is related, perhaps indirectly but almost as strongly as is Theseus' great speech, to the Boethian norm defined in the metrum ending:

> O felix hominum genus,
> Si vestros animos amor
> Quo caelum regitur regat.
> (*De consolatione,* 2. Met. 8)

Which thought, in turn, relates to the main thought of Plato's *Timaeus.*

The main lines have now been laid down for an interpretation of the puzzling features of *Epithalamion* described in the first two chapters: (1) symbolizing the day in the number of stanzas and the year in the number of long lines, Spenser indicates the main points of the sun's progress during the year by a system of stanza-matching and contrasting refrains which indicate the positions of the starry sphere and the periods of light and darkness at those seasonal points; (2) symbolizing simultaneously the daily and annual movements of the sun in relation to the regions of the

---

[7] In *The Allegory of Love* (Oxford, 1938).
[8] In *The Parlement of Foules* (Oxford, 1957).

sidereal hours in the sphere of the fixed stars, he indicates at the
end of the poem that particular disparity of this relationship at the
daily level which induces the annual movement, through which,
in turn, the seasons and the variations in the daily durations of
light and darkness are induced. The two sets of symbolism thus
correspond to each other. By all of this he signifies that microcosmic-macrocosmic consolation by which our pathetic, individual,
temporal and spatial imperfection is seen as only one aspect of a
paradoxical strength by which we as humans, through marriage
and generation, partake in the cyclical harmony of an according
whole, although this mutation-filled perfection must finally yield
place to the immutable perfection of God's Eternity.

Much, however, remains to be shown. In the envoy, in particular, certain obscurities remain for which the present theory affords no clear answer. What are the "ornaments" which the
song is made in lieu of? Does the "cutting off" apply to them or
to the song? If to them, does Spenser mean that the song itself
has cut them off? To this class of questions the answers here must
be tentative, although this uncertainty does not, as far as can be
seen, affect the validity of the theory already presented.

It may be that these ornaments are merely presents which did
not arrive in time, either because of an external accident or because the date of the wedding was unexpectedly advanced, as has
often been suggested. Much weight, however, may be attached to
the alternative theory of Professor Alexander C. Judson: [9]

Spenser begins his *Epithalamion* with a reference to the poems he has
written to "adorne" others, and he ends it with the statement that this
hymn was written "in lieu of many ornaments." . . . It is natural to
assume that by "ornaments" he meant "poems." Since his sonnet cycle
ends abruptly in misunderstanding and separation, may we not suppose
that he intended to round it out with additional sonnets, but for some
unexplained reason determined to compose his great marriage hymn
instead?

[9] *The Life of Edmund Spenser* (Baltimore, 1945), p. 172.

Amoretti and *Epithalamion* were, of course, first published as one volume. In *Amoretti* 69, which is closest in wording (although not in depth of meaning) to the envoy of *Epithalamion*, Spenser speaks, in a familiar conceit, of the trophies erected by generals of the Ancient World to commemorate their victories, and of ·how "this verse" (i.e., the sonnet), "vowd to eternity," will be the "immortal moniment" of his "loves conquest." As in this case, so in others, Spenser would have been following a familiar Petrarchan habit in thinking of his sonnets as a series of adorn- ·ments or ornaments, so that there is nothing intrinsically unlikely about Professor Judson's notion. In addition, reason has been shown above for supposing that Spenser, seeing his poem in one sense as a cyclical enactment of the day and the year, would have reason to suggest its beginning in its end: consequently the empha- sis on adornment in the first stanza and "ornaments" in the last stanza as referring especially to poems seems apt. According to this interpretation, the literal meaning of the envoy would be: "Song, made· as a substitute for the sonnets which would have completed the sequence my bride deserves—which sonnets you, (1) cutting them off through the hasty accidents which prevented me from completing them, now step in to replace before your due time in the total plan of composition which I originally intended; but (2) being, as you are, also promised as a recompense both for· the missing sonnets and for the fact that you are out of due or- der—rise to the responsibility of being a sufficient poem to adorn her and be (as they are) an eternal monument to her through all time." The meaning which I have already assigned to some of these lines would then be an allegorical one imposed upon the literal one, and the extreme obscurity of the passage would be par- tially explained by Spenser's effort to cover two disparate mean- ings. at once within very short compass. But the literal interpreta- tion here remains speculative, although it has much to recom- mend it. In addition, the notion that Spenser's obscurity here is due to an effort to compress multiple meanings into one short stanza is capable of further development.

This further development may most easily be approached by considering various possible meanings of the epithet "short time" in the last line. Fairly obviously, it implies at least two things: that the song is an eternal monument throughout all time, until the end of the world; and that the song is also a monument for a particular short time—the wedding day—in accordance with the familiar Renaissance notion that poetry eternizes those events or persons which it celebrates. Equally obviously, if the main interpretation I have provided is a correct one, the poem is a monument to short time in the sense that it celebrates the cyclical measures of time created by the sun—the day, the year, and their divisions; and in the sense that it celebrates short time over against Eternity. But there is also a variety of senses in which *Epithalamion* might be thought of as a monument to short time in the sense of time caught short, or time which is too short for a particular purpose. It is, for instance, a monument to the time of the sidereal day, which is too short for a complete orbit of the sun, this incompleteness being one of the main points of the symbolism. But there are other possible ways in which this particular meaning may have been useful to Spenser. All of them are put forward here tentatively, for I see no way of surely demonstrating that he did, or did not, intend them. Others may find such grounds; and, in any case, plurality of meanings forms a possible explanation of Spenser's obscurity in this passage.

The first of these possible ways would have permitted him to excuse a diurnal discrepancy. It has already been pointed out that the main time signification of the stanzas seems to be as sidereal hours—regions in the sky and time measures of the stars' movement—not solar hours of the solar day. Consequently these stanzas do not have to be coordinated with the sun's diurnal progress, and they need not correspond exactly to the hourly measurement of

the literally described events of the day of the marriage. Nevertheless they do both these things approximately, according, apparently,
to Spenser's intention; and for the failure of the sun to arrive at
its 359th degree of daily movement in the twenty-fourth hour of
the day instead of the twenty-third he may have thought that he
needed some excuse. The excuse is obviously available in yet another meaning of the envoy: the song arrives before its due time
in the sense that, symbolizing the movement of the sun, it arrives at
359° at the end of the twenty-third stanza hour instead of in the
twenty-fourth, and in this fashion the song is (somewhat whim-
sically) a monument to time caught short, although the *tornata*
forms a "recompense" in the sense that it provides the alternative
measure of the year.

A second way in which "short time" as "time caught short"
may have served Spenser's symbolic schemes must also be put forward tentatively. Just as the "recompensing" function of the
envoy may have been intended to take care of a diurnal discrepancy, it may also have seemed to Spenser to cover what he may
have considered an annual one. It will be remembered that the
region of each celestial hour encompasses fifteen degrees, and that
the sun passes through each of the regions in between fifteen and
sixteen days; it will also be remembered, however, that Spenser
found it necessary to supply a larger number of stanzas with sixteen long lines (instead of fifteen) than symmetry required, since
he wished to reach long line 359 precisely at the end of stanza
23. But in addition to symbolizing degrees of the sun's progress and
days of the year by these long lines, Spenser may conceivably have
had in mind to symbolize each of the twelve months by two stanzas
each, which would have been approximately suitable: a month of
thirty days could be signified by two stanzas containing fifteen long
lines each; a month of thirty-one days, by one stanza of fifteen
long lines and another of sixteen. Each stanza would then suggest
approximately a fortnight. If he had any such plan, however, it

would be thwarted by the necessity, on grounds already indicated, of having fourteen stanzas of sixteen long lines each, although there are but seven months of thirty-one days each. If, for example, he started his poem with March (as he did the procession of the months in the Mutability Cantos; in addition, starting with this month, the arithmetic of *Epithalamion* comes closest to the theorized intention), then at the end of the first part of February (stanza 23), he would find himself with six days in hand. He could at this point excuse himself in the envoy in the way that has already been indicated for the diurnal discrepancy. Additional reasons will be put forward in the next chapter for supposing that Spenser may have intended the course of his poem to follow the seasonal events of a year, beginning in March, as, at the literal level, he followed the arc of the day; but this conclusion, too, must be regarded as highly tentative.

A third way in which "short time" may have been intended as "time caught short" is probably the most speculative of all, but it deserves to be put forward, if for nothing else, then for its amusement value. It is Metaphysically frivolous and may be considered dangerously un-Spenserian, but the possibility that Spenser intended it remains, in what is after all a very jovial poem. To understand it we must recollect several points. In stanza 15, in what, literally, is the only example of fescennine humor in *Epithalamion*, Spenser divulges to the young men of the town that for his marriage the longest night and the shortest day would be most appropriate, not the other way around. In stanza 20, during the marriage night, we are told that "it will soone be day." But literally, at the end of stanza 23, as though he were unconscious of the approach of light, the poet urges his bride to rest after a period during which the lovers have been conscious of little but their "paradise of joyes" (l. 366). Symbolically, however, at this point the sun has passed through 359° of its daily movement. What, now, would happen if we conceived of the remaining six long lines (those of the envoy)

not simply as days of the year or degrees of the sun's annual movement, but also as degrees of the sun's daily progress, like the preceding long lines? Evidently the sun would complete its circle in
the first line of the envoy and then rise five degrees above the
horizon, into a new day. If Spenser in fact wished to excuse this
scandalous discrepancy, the envoy would perform a new recompensing function: the "short time" of the night of the summer
solstice ends before the "dew time" that the poet formerly expressed himself as preferring for his wedding night; the sun rises
upon the surprised lovers, the bride now being without her due
ornaments, but a recompense is provided in terms of the alternative
time measurement of the poem, whereby the sun does not rise at
all, but only the year is symbolized. The conceit itself, whereby
the sun rises but does not rise, offers no difficulty; it is simply a
variant on a familiar group, like Marlowe's in *Hero and Leander:*

> And now the sun that through th'horizon peeps,
> As pitying these lovers, downward creeps,
>
> (99–100)

or Donne's (from *The Sun Rising*):

> Thy beams, so reverend and strong
> Why shouldst thou think?
> I could eclipse and cloud them with a wink.

Yet another sense in which the envoy may perform a recompensing function will be examined in the next chapter.

IV. THE SHORT LINES: THE YEAR

Was never so great joyance since the day,
That all the gods whylome assembled were,
On *Hæmus* hill in their divine array,
To celebrate the solemne bridall cheare,
Twixt *Peleus,* and dame *Thetis* pointed there;
Where *Phoebus* self, that god of Poets hight,
They say did sing the spousall hymne full cleere,
That all the gods were ravisht with delight
Of his celestiall song, and Musicks wondrous might.

(Faerie Queene 7.7.12)

The investigation up to this point has led through several stages. It was necessary to show clearly and unmistakably in the first two chapters the existence in *Epithalamion* of two complexes of symbolism, and to show also that interpretation of them was called for, since they had in themselves little or no perceptible relation to the general intent of the poem. The interpretation followed, in accordance with features of Spenser's thought on which there is general agreement, and was, to a degree, self-checking: one complex could be seen to relate to the other in a very satisfactory fashion for purposes of demonstration, so that this interpretation seems, as the old astronomers said, to "save the appearances" in this small creation.

There remain, however, certain other problems of interpretation—one of them of considerable poetic import—to which no such self-checking answers can be given. I have endeavored to find reasonable answers to these unavoidable problems, but no sure demonstration seems to me possible.

The most immediate of these problems, because it is internal

to the symbolism already discussed, is that of the short lines. It is
first necessary to recall from Chapter I an assumption from which
the discussion led to the independently valid discovery of the total
of 365 long lines in *Epithalamion*. It was pointed out there that
the division between daylight and darkness part of the way through
stanza 17 agreed with the division between daylight and darkness
on the day and in the latitude of the marriage, in the sense that
the division corresponded to sixteen and a fraction hours of daylight, and seven and a fraction of darkness. The possibility was
then raised of a further refinement in this particular time indication.
Spenser shows night actually arriving in the fifth line of the
seventeenth stanza, at the end of the first of four groups of long
lines in this stanza. The demarcations between the groups are made
by three short lines, as in most of the other stanzas. Now, supposing that Spenser had accepted the figure of sixteen and one-quarter
hours of daylight for this day at the northern edge of the seventh
clime, as given in the *De sphaera* of Johannes de Sacrobosco and
in *The Kalender of Shepherdes,* the conclusion would follow that
he had fractionized his seventeenth stanza accordingly, so that the
first group of long lines symbolized the last quarter hour of daylight, and the other three groups stood in like fashion for the three
quarters of an hour at the beginning of the period of seven and
three-quarter hours of darkness, according to the figure in *De
sphaera* and *The Kalendar.* One possible implication of this was
described as being that the long lines signified duration of time, and
the short lines divisions of time. From this possibility the discussion
moved in Chapter I to the discovery that the total number of long
lines in the poem was 365, and at that point in the exposition this
independently valuable datum was all that was needed. It is now
necessary, however, to investigate the grounds and consequences
of the assumption that, in terms of time, as the long lines signify
duration, so the short lines signify divisions.

A reader may well demand at this point whether there is really something here to explain, and whether, in fact, it is likely that Spenser desired to give any time-mensurating value at all to these short lines: perhaps they are nothing but the free punctuations of the lyrical flow that they are seen to be at first reading. Yet in a poem of 24 stanzas and 365 long lines, containing indications of the four seasonal points by a complex system of divisions and matchings of the total number of stanzas, and defining the relation of the sidereal day to the year in its envoy, this is unlikely to be the case; we cannot save the appearances at all if we remain satisfied with the notion that Spenser may not have operated with similar logicality and *Gründlichkeit* in the matter of his short lines. Furthermore, the theory of interpretation which I offer tentatively below affords a reasonable explanation for two details in the poem which have always puzzled editors—the omission of one short line where it would normally be expected in stanza 15 and of another in stanza 23. The theory which I describe below depends on the general assumption that Spenser placed his short lines so as to symbolize divisions of time at both the diurnal and annual level, just as his long lines signify duration of time at these two levels, but that (as with the long lines) satisfying these two demands leads him into a compromise which he wittily excuses through conceits. That this conception involves difficulties I should be the first to admit; even so, it quite possibly mirrors Spenser's intention.

The first difficulty concerns stanza 17 itself. If Spenser actually accepted the figure of sixteen and one quarter, and embodied it in this stanza, then he chose a value which would be proper if he had been married in Torquay, but is about half an hour too short for a marriage in Kilcolman, Cork, or Youghal. If he had located nightfall at a point signifying sixteen and three-quarter hours of daylight instead of sixteen and one-quarter, he would have hit the true value to the nearest minute for the latitude of Cork at the summer solstice, and it is in the cathedral of that city that his marriage to Elizabeth Boyle has sometimes been supposed to have occurred. In fact the long line immediately preceding the third short line of stanza 17 (in other words, the concluding line of the third group of long lines in this stanza, and consequently sixteen and three-quarters hours after sunrise according to the interpretation provided here) suggests at first glance that night is just falling: "Now it is night, ye damsels may be gon." But the pertinent clause here seems to be adverbial, i.e., "Now *that* it is night," etc. This easy way out, then, is not available, and would entail in any case the infelicity of dedicating to night, by means of the first negative refrain, a stanza which is three-quarters day. The decisive point really seems to come earlier in the stanza, as indicated, at the fifth line ("Now night is come, now soone her disaray"), which follows two lines after "Now day is doen, and night is nighing fast," in a kind of progression.

The difficulty in question really concerns the perpetuation of an ancient error. The *De sphaera* of Johannes de Sacrobosco (thought to be British) indicates that there are seven habitable climes and gives the value of sixteen and one-quarter hours of daylight for the longest day of the year at the northern edge of the seventh and northernmost regularly habitable clime. *The Kalender of Shepherdes* follows this tradition, and both works were read by generations of Englishmen in the Renaissance and after. Spenser probably knew the *De sphaera*, and he was certainly acquainted with *The Kalender*, because it is one of his models for *The Shepheardes Calender*. The *De sphaera* adds [1] that there is no further clime beyond the seventh because living conditions to the north are so difficult—"quoniam prave est habitationis." But according to this work the northern edge of the seventh clime extends

---

[1] *The* Sphere *of Sacrobosco and Its Commentators* (ed. Lynn Thorndike, Chicago, 1949), p. 140.

only to 50°30′ North Latitude, and Robert the Englishman had already militantly pointed out [2] in the second half of the thirteenth century that this figure excludes most of England; in fact it excludes all of the British Isles but the southern parts of Cornwall and Devonshire.

Would Spenser himself have accepted the figure of sixteen and one quarter, even if many of his countrymen did? Learned contemporaries of his did not,[3] and there are other sources,[4] apart from the difficult matter of personal observation, from which he could have derived a figure closer to the truth. Nevertheless, there may have been reasons for his making use of it, among which ignorance is not necessarily an item. The advantage of mirroring a celestial phenomenon in an earthly one seems to me to have been the strongest of these reasons, in a poem where the analogy between the heavens and man's life is so important. Just as the sun has reached the northernmost point of its annual journey on the summer solstice, the day of the marriage, so the groom might be

[2] Thorndike, p. 187.

[3] In his long commentary, printed at Lyons in 1577 (*Fr. Ivnctini Florentini . . . Commentaria in Spaeram Ioannis de Sacro Bosco, Lugduni, apud Phillipum Tinghium*), Iunctinus, or Giuntini, quotes the relevant passage from Sacrobosco concerning the seventh clime (with the value of 16¼ hours), and then explains: Octavvm Ptolemaeus non posuit: cum illud terrae (quodcunque est) ipsi incognitum a neotericis lustratum sit (III, section entitled "De divisione climatum," p. 215). Towards the end of this section he adds: Astrologi moderni ex Germania, & Anglia octauum clima addiderunt, ne regiones illae extra climata remanerent. Regiones autem ultra septimum clima sunt istae, Hibernia insula, Albion insula, vbi & Anglia, & Scotia, & plures aliae prouinciae positae sunt, etc. (p. 217). He gives no value for the period of daylight in this eighth clime.

[4] He might, for instance, have consulted a sheet-almanac drawn up for London. Thomas Buckminster's, for the year 1595, yields the average value of 16 hrs., 26 mins., for the period between sunrise and sunset on a day in June: "Sunne riseth at iij a clocke/ and xlvij. minutes,/ Setteth at viij./ and xiij minutes." The fragment of this almanac from which this comes is reproduced as Plate XXVI in Eustace F. Bosanquet, *English Printed Almanacs and Prognostications . . . to the Year 1600* (London, 1917).

supposed to have reached the high point of his mortal life in marriage; after the procreation referred to in stanzas 22 and 23, the
importance of the parent begins to decline, just as the sun, after
this high point, "somewhat loseth of his heat and light" (l. 268).
Thus, to celebrate one's marriage on the day when the sun reaches
the northernmost point of its annual journey is exciting, but to
locate this celebration at the northern edge of the seventh and
traditionally northernmost habitable clime might well be thought
overwhelming, because both locations express in a manner the
extreme limit of those departures from a more perfect standard by
which the uncertain glories of Short Time are attained. Spenser
may also have been expressing his conservatism: poetry should be
generated from the immemorial testimony of ancient wisdom, and
this particular figure of sixteen and one quarter, as he may have
known, was a Ptolemaic datum emanating finally from Hellen-
istic Egypt: "Et infinita annorum millia in solis Aegyptiorum
monumentis librisque releguntur." [5]

The difficulty, however, must not be minimized. But unless
Spenser proceeded in the way that I have described, I do not see
how any logical explanation can be found for the symbolic role of
the short lines, which seem obviously contrasted in role, as well
as in length, to the long ones. The purpose that he made them
serve may have been marginal to his design, but once it is granted
that the long lines signify duration at the annual level, it is necessary for us to suppose that Spenser gave a contrasting role to his
short lines, so as to call forth a harmonious symbolic music, like
an undersong, accompanying the remarkable audible music of the
Epithalamion-stanza. I suppose him to have conceived each of his
stanzas as symbolizing the actual substance of time—of an hour—
through its numbers (cf. l. 280, "How slowly do the houres theyr
numbers spend?"), so that in each of the stanzas so divided he sets
up the auditory image of elapsing quarter hours, punctuated by the

[5] Macrobius, *Commentarius ex Cicerone in somnium Scipionis.* 2.10.

tripping sound of trimeters and ending at the hour with the word
"ring." It is not necessary, of course, that the actual events of the
marriage day should follow this scheme, each in its own quarter
hour, but the reader is often made to feel the slow unfolding of
events through these stanzas (as, for instance, in stanzas 16 and
17), so that what happens is not described as having happened, but
as though only just occurring.

Logically speaking, however, Spenser would find himself bound
to express an annual significance through these short lines as well
as a diurnal one of quarter-hourly divisions, just as the long lines
possess symbolically both diurnal and annual duration. However,
in seeking divisions of the year which would correspond in number
to divisions of the day (as the degrees of the sun's progress daily
and annually are made to correspond in terms of long lines),
Spenser would have found himself in difficulties; but it is possible
to imagine (although not to prove) how his resolution of these
difficulties would have forced him to omit one long line each in
stanzas 15 and 23.

His difficulty would have consisted in the fact that there is no
one class of divisions of the year that comes near the total needed
for signifying at the other level the quarter-hourly divisions of the
day. We may construct a theoretical chain of reasoning, however,
which would bring him to his final solution as expressed in the
poem: faced with the difficulty, he hits upon the notion of the short
lines in their annual significance as a procession of *various classes*
of divisions of the year, passing through the poem somewhat in
the way in which so many processions are represented in *The
Faerie Queene*, especially the procession of the divisions of the year
in the Mutability Cantos. But he cannot use quite the same per-
sonnel as in that procession: Seasons, Months, Day and Night, the
Hours, and Life and Death. Life and Death are out of the question: for many they do not fall generally within the limit of a
year, and, more importantly, the succession of the generations is

already the subject matter of the poem. The Hours and Day and Night are likewise excluded as candidates for representation by short lines, for they are taken care of at the daily level of signification, and it is the annual level with which he is now concerned. Remaining, then, are the Seasons and Months, but their total of sixteen is far less than the number he needs. He consequently adds the final class of annual divisions, the weeks, which are not lacking in poetic dignity—they are, after all, honored in *Les semaines* of Du Bartas, whom Spenser evidently considered the only worthy successor of Du Bellay in France (cf. *The Ruines of Rome*, ll. 459–62).[6] On this total he settles, because it is close enough to his other intention. But not quite congruent with it, since to supply three short lines per stanza, for quarter-hourly divisions, he would need a total of 72, and the total of the seasons, months, and weeks is only 68.[7] He decides on a compromise according to which the short lines become only a dominant auditory image of quarter-hourly divisions, carried through in most of the stanzas, but not all; accordingly he finds natural or artful ways of omitting four of the diurnally required 72, so that he may end with the annual requirement of 68.

Of these four necessary omissions, two are cared for in the envoy, which contains only one short line instead of the usual three. Another omission occurs in stanza 15, where Spenser plays on the concept "shortest-longest." In my view he plays on it not simply in terms of the subject matter of this stanza, but also in its form. It is the shortest of the regular stanzas, containing but

[6] Cf. here the somewhat distantly applicable comment of Harry Berger, Jr. (*The Allegorical Temper* . . . , New Haven, 1957, p. 96, note), on Spenser's apparent modification of his sources so as to make Ebranck's sons equal in number to the weeks of the year (*Faerie Queene* 2.10.22.): "The number of offspring are now related to nature's annual cycle."

[7] The annual significance of this total was first excogitated by Mr. Elliot Roberts, ten minutes after exposure to the problem in an undergraduate seminar. I am indebted to him.

seventeen lines, but where the second short line would normally be expected, Spenser writes "To chose the *longest* day in all the yeare" (my italics), thus wittily excusing the superficial departure from stanzaic symmetry and also giving us, in a stanza shorter than the other regular ones, a long line in place of a short one.

The fourth of the omissions treated here occurs in stanza 23. Line 424, "So let us rest, sweet love, in hope of this," would normally be followed by the third short line of the stanza, rhyming with "this." This short line does not appear, so that the reader is forced to be satisfied with the rhyme "happinesse," six lines above. This is so drastic that editors have supposed the printer accidentally to have dropped a line. No such explanation is necessary, however, if we suppose that Spenser defies our normal expectation of a short line here so as to create a situation that can be "recompensed" in his *tornata,* in accordance with his manner of resolving his other symbolic schemes: just as the poem seems to end in its twenty-third stanza with the incomplete circle of the sun symbolized by the 359 long lines, so its conclusion seems to be embarrassed as well by the lack of the last of the sixty-eight divisions of the year, or, alternatively, by the lack of a quarter-hour mark—this lack not being wittily excused as in stanza 15. But this symbolic lack at the annual level and the purely formal lack of the short line itself in the twenty-third stanza are triumphantly "recompensed" by the short line "But promist both to recompens" in the *tornata,* so that the year is made complete in terms of the short lines as well as the long ones.

The reader will decide for himself whether judgment's better part consists in entertaining the above theory, so as to extend Spenser's apparent scheme to its logical conclusion, or in passing over the question, where so much must depend on hypothesis. To the present writer it seems that the theory is justified in its fruits, since it provides an explanation for the previously puzzling and apparently inexplicable omission of lines where they would normally be expected. There is, however, yet another discrepancy in the matter of these short lines, for which I can offer nothing but speculation: the last short line in stanza 1 and the only short line in stanza 24 are tetrameters, although all the rest of the short lines are trimeters. Perhaps Spenser wished to suggest in this way a connection between his first stanza and his last, so as to confirm the poem's cyclical, recurrent symbolism, but this must remain pure conjecture.

More important than the problem of the short lines, because it concerns the poetic impact of *Epithalamion* in a more extensive way, is the question whether Spenser extended his symbolism of the course of the year to express the qualities of the seasons and of seasonal change, as well as simply signifying the duration of 365 steps in the sun's annual progress. It is possible that he intended the course of his poem to represent covertly the arc of the rising and descending year as he literally represents that of the day. But the application of Occam's razor to the subject matter of the poem forces upon us the conclusion that this simultaneous operation can never surely be proved, because the activities which here suggest to the imagination spring, summer, autumn, and winter are ones which, one by one, Spenser would have been expected to take up in the course of describing a wedding day according to the epithalamial tradition.

There is, however, a statistical reason to support one who reads imaginatively the course of the seasons in the poem. It is not one which we have already suggested: in Chapter II, the point was made that if Spenser had intended to symbolize the course of each of the twelve months by two stanzas each, then the arithmetical discrepancy which has to be "recompensed" in the envoy would be least if the poem were conceived as starting with March, as the procession of months did in the Mutability Cantos. This can really be given little weight, since it is not plain on the basis of what has been shown that Spenser had any intention of symbolizing the months by two stanzas each. What is striking, however, is the arithmetical position in the poem of two obvious mentions of the "day"—ostensibly the day of the marriage. According to the testimony of the poem, this day was June 11, St. Barnabas' Day in Spenser's Julian Calendar. It is the 103rd day from March 1. As we suppose, the days of the year are symbolized in *Epithalamion* by long lines. The following quotation gives long lines 101–5, with a concluding short line:

> O fayrest Phoebus, father of the Muse,
> If ever I did honour thee aright,
> Or sing the thing, that mote thy mind delight,
> Doe not thy servants simple boone refuse,
> But let this day let this one day be myne,
> Let all the rest be thine.

That is to say, the sun as the creator of days may have all the others, but Spenser, as the servant of the father of the Muse, implores that this one day may be given to him. The important point, obviously, is that the marriage day—the 103rd day of the year, reckoning this year as beginning with March 1—is included in the sentence in which Spenser asks to have "this day" for himself, as though he were specifying the particular line corresponding to it. Admittedly, the evidence would be more impressive if the word itself had fallen in the 103rd long line, instead of the 105th, but the location of the sentence as a whole carries considerable weight, especially when one realizes that references to the "day" are not really numerous in this poem. One other such reference seems equally significant.

    March 1 is not, of course, conventionally speaking, the first day of the year, which for Elizabethans was Lady Day, March 25— the day of the Annunciation, giving to man, through the promise of the Redeemer, the hope of a new life which will replace the old one of sin and death. Long lines 25–30, with an interpolated short line, follow:

> Bid her awake therefore and soone her dight,
> For lo the wished day is come at last,
> That shall for al the paynes and sorrowes past,
> Pay to her usury of long delight:
> And whylest she doth her dight,
> Doe ye to her of joy and solace sing,
> That all the woods may answer and your eccho ring.

That is to say, literally, the day of the wedding has arrived, in which a new life of love will open, in accordance with Spenser's so often expressed view of the two sides of love—one painful, the other harmonious (cf. particularly the hymns *Of Love* and *Of Beautie*). But these lines would as fittingly describe the coming of the new year. In *Amoretti* Spenser describes, with frequent calendrical references, about two years of arduous courtship. On each of two New Year's Days he looks forward in hope to the coming year (*Amoretti* 4, 62); in these lines from his ode, he may be announcing the fruition of his hope at the beginning of the year in which his marriage occurs. Furthermore, the religious significance which I have implied these lines may possess would seem to Spenser's eyes to combine in perfect propriety with the idea of his own mortal love: if any proof of this were needed, his sonnet for Easter (*Amoretti* 68) would provide it.

These two references to the day, then, would cover both the beginning of the year, and the day of Spenser's marriage: and the time units of the year and the day, as we have already tried to show, are symbolized by the whole of *Epithalamion*. There are only two other references to the quality of the day in the poem. One of them, in stanza 14 (ll. 246–49), matches the above-quoted lines from stanza 2; it seems to have no further significance than to underline the equivalence according to the scheme of matching stanzas outlined in Chapter II. It is a precursor, however, of the fourth mention of the day, in stanza 15, in several ways a key stanza, in which Spenser comes closest to making his symbolic purpose plain. It is the stanza which announces the date of the marriage as the longest day in the year, St. Barnabas' Day, and which, playing on the concepts of the longest and shortest days in the year, is the shortest of the regular stanzas, but also contains a long line in place of a short one. It is also the only stanza which not only closes, but opens, with the word "ring"; in it, the young men of the town are urged to ring bells to make the day wear away, which appears to be the equivalent of the singing of "this song" by the Muses in the matching stanza 3, for the stanzas of "this song" represent hours of the day, each but the last ending with the word "ring." All of this being the case, it seems appropriate for Spenser to speak in this key stanza of the day explicitly, without the necessity of its being related to a putative scheme whereby two important dates (i.e., New Year's Day and the day of the marriage) may be built into the structure of the poem elsewhere.

The evidence for Spenser's having actually intended this latter is in sum, however, inconclusive. Despite the striking coincidence that one sentence memorializing the "day" corresponds in this schedule to the date of New Year, and that another corresponds to the actual date of the marriage, the fact that there are two other mentions of the day without any apparent important correspondences in terms of this scheme forces a reservation of judgment.

This part of the argument, then, cannot give much help in the related question with which we started: does Spenser symbolize the seasonal events of the year at the same time that he describes the events of the day? The view is a very seductive one that the arc of the poem follows the arc of the rising and declining year from March onwards—from the tentative awakening of the Muses in the damp before sunrise, through the awakening of the bride with the sound of birdsong among the dewy leaves, the request to the sun not to shine hotly, the marriage itself, and the feast like a harvest festival, to the retirement into the majesty of night from which new life may arise (like the retirement of organic life in winter); but it is a view which I find no sure way of defending, because of the Occamite considerations previously raised. The strongest evidence that can be adduced is by analogy. *Amoretti* 70, in which spring, the herald of love, is told to go "to my love, where she is carelesse layd,/ Yet in her winters bowre not well awake," and warn her to take time by the forelock, seems to be related in terms of its conceit to *Amoretti* 4, in which the new year calls forth "out of sad Winters night,/ Fresh love, that long hath slept in cheerlesse bower." In both sonnets the conceit seems to consist in the fact that the rising from a night's sleep is equated with the awakening from the long sleep of winter, as in the case of so much of organic nature. Both the beloved (in 70) and Love (in 4) are to awake to the spring (70.9: "lusty spring now in his timely howre"), and in 70 the time of the season is equated with the time of day (70.13: "Make hast therefore sweet love, whilest it is prime"). It seems very likely that in stanza 5 of *Epithalamion* (which would represent the first half of May according to the present scheme) the call to the bride to come forth from what has been called her "bowre" (l. 23) to the accompaniment of birdsong among the dewy leaves is similarly seasonal, and that the retirement into the "boures" (l. 299) in stanza 17 (at the beginning of November) may also stand for the retirement of organic life into the seedbed of winter; but I see no way to prove this.

With one exception,[8] I find that further speculation about time

---

[8] In the sense that to one possibility a fairly sure negative answer may be given. In the penultimate stanza of the Mutability Cantos, "Short *Time* shall soon cut down with his consuming sickle" the "flowring pride" of (finally) vain life. In *Faerie Queene* 3.6.39, in the Garden of Adonis, the enemy of the effort of life to maintain itself is "wicked Time," who with his scythe mows down "the flowring herbes" of the garden. Spenser thus twice used the image of Time cutting down "flowering" symbols of life. The possi-

symbolism in *Epithalamion* strikes a point of declining returns. Consequently the course of interpretation may be terminated here.

---

bility may be raised that the "short time" of the last line of *Epithalamion*, along with the accompanying reminders of mortality over against eternity, was memorialized, in a kind of self-mortifying symbol, in the ornamental borders at the top and bottom of the pages of the first edition of *Amoretti and Epithalamion* (1595); but I do not think the notion can be shown to possess much likelihood. The design is composed of fleurons enclosed in sickles, as though the sickles were cutting vegetation. It will be remembered that the stanzas of *Epithalamion* are divided by a change of refrain into sixteen stanzas representing day and eight stanzas representing night. There are sixteen sickles in each lower border in the British Museum copy (facsimile published by Noel Douglas, London, 1927), but in the upper border there are, alas, nine, not eight, except on the last page, where there are eight. But this latter is probably a mistake, since the eight are arranged unsymmetrically so as to suggest a missing ninth. The Folger Museum copy shows the same variations, as my friend Mr. John Hammond was kind enough to ascertain. In view of the description in the Variorum (*Minor Poems*, II, 697, 698) of the correction of sheets, it is unlikely that any of the other extant copies of this edition would show much variation in the numbers of the sickles. The number of units in the lower border was most probably dictated by the size of the page and by the size of the blocks which the printer, Peter Short, had at his disposal for the design.

Apart from the unlikelihood that the sickles correspond to the Hours of Day and Night, the more general possibility that the sickles were chosen expressly as reminders of mortality and short time is weakened by the consideration that approximately the same basic design, built up of small blocks, is used rather frequently by sixteenth-century printers in setting up ornamental borders. Cf. Henry R. Plomer, *English Printers' Ornaments* (London, 1924), Plate 19 (a border by Bynneman for *The Palace of Pleasure*, II, 1567), Plate 86 (a tailpiece by Jugge for *The Book of Common Prayer*, 1573), and the description of these plates; see also Plates II and III, and the references to fleurons in the index. A design resembling the lower border in *Amoretti and Epithalamion*, 1595, is also used, for headpieces and a tailpiece, in Spenser and Gabriel Harvey's *Three Proper, and Wittie, familiar Letters*, 1580, printed by Bynneman. The most easily available reproductions of these, and of the title page of *Epithalamion*, showing the borders, are in Smith and De Selincourt's *Poetical Works of Edmund Spenser* (Oxford, 1912). The apparently significant design in the center of this title page is simply the printer's mark of Peter Short, used by him elsewhere.

CONCLUSION

The old Church knew best the enduring needs of man,
beyond the spasmodic needs of today and yesterday . . . .
the religious and ritualistic rhythm of the year, in human
life. . . . Mankind has got to get back to the rhythm of
the cosmos, and the permanence of marriage.

(D. H. Lawrence)

I have not found a source for Spenser's special technique of symbolism in *Epithalamion*. It is true that the derivation of other special features of this adventure in the realm of time offers no problem: the elaborate, mythologizing association of the movements
of the heavens with the life of man, for instance, is perhaps best
exemplified in "Le quatriesme jour" of *La Première Sepmaine* of
Guillaume Du Bartas, where Spenser admired it,[1] but it is a feature of many other Renaissance verse and prose works. Furthermore every item of the astronomical knowledge which Spenser
would have needed for his symbolism was so widely distributed
among the educated that it is not necessary to cite a source, except
perhaps in the matter of the Hours, on which I include an appendix. Even such a tyro in the advanced theoretical astronomy
of his day as Gabriel Harvey and F. R. Johnson[2] make Spenser
out to be would have had no trouble in coming by it. But the fact
remains that I have found no analogue for his devices of creating
significance through the totals of the stanzas and of the long and
short lines, and through the matching of stanzas in series.

[1] See *Gabriel Harvey's Marginalia*, ed. G. C. Moore Smith (Stratford-
upon-Avon, 1913), p. 161.
[2] *Astronomical Thought in Renaissance England* (Baltimore, 1937), pp.
193–95, where Harvey's remark from the *Marginalia* is quoted.

Examples of the class to which these devices belong can be easily given. Spenser himself displays a penchant for simple numerical organization in some of his other poems, although not surely for numerical symbolism except in the well-known cases of the twelve months of *The Shepheardes Calender* and the twelve virtues in twelve books of *The Faerie Queene* as planned. *The Ruines of Time*, *Daphnaida*, and *The Teares of the Muses* all display verified, although not yet completely understood, signs of numerical organization.[3] In addition, many Middle Latin poems are organized on complicated principles of arithmetical symmetry; medieval vernacular works, according to the results of some recent research,[4] are sometimes so organized; and it is a matter of general knowledge that the *Divina Commedia* is numerically organized. In the other arts such organization is a well-known feature; it may be pointed out, for instance, that Knole, owned (but not inhabited until 1603) by Thomas Sackville, Lord Buckhurst, in the later days of Elizabeth I, allegedly contains seven courtyards, 52 staircases, and 365 rooms.[5] But one looks for something more precise than this kind of evidence—something closer to Spenser's

---

[3] See Variorum *Minor Poems*, III, 530, note; I, 440–44, note; II, 542, note; E. R. Curtius, *European Literature and the Latin Middle Ages* (New York, 1953), p. 508. Perhaps the best explanation of the scheme in *The Teares of the Muses* is that Spenser invokes the nine Muses in the first nine stanzas and then devotes ten stanzas to each of the Muses' plaints successively, except that he feels constrained to give Euterpe an extra, eleventh stanza so as to arrive at the round total of 100 stanzas.

[4] For medieval Latin as well as vernacular verse, cf. E. R. Curtius, *European Literature and the Latin Middle Ages*, pp. 501–9 ("Numerical Composition"). A large number of studies having to do with numerical organization of vernacular works have recently appeared; cf., for example, A. T. Hatto, "On Beauty of Numbers in Wolfram's Dawn Songs," *Modern Language Review*, XLV (1950), 181–88; J. A. Huisman, *Neue Wege zur dichterischen und musikalischen Technik Walthers von der Vogelweide, mit einem Exkurs über die symmetrische Zahlenkomposition im Mittelalter* (Utrecht, 1950).

[5] V. Sackville-West, *Knole and the Sackvilles* (London, 1922), p. 4.

practice, among the Latin, Italian, French, or English verse that he is likely to have read, or some contemporary exposition of the purposes, means, and advantages of such a symbolizing method. I have looked in vain.

It is difficult to know where to turn in a field not yet systematically studied. It may be that among the hundreds of Latin and vernacular epithalamia which Spenser might have read [6] some analogue will yet turn up; my search has certainly not been exhaustive, and specialists in the relevant literatures may be able, in time, to provide light. Among English marriage odes only one with which I am acquainted could be suspected of a connection with Spenser's in terms of the symbolism discussed in this book. Ben Jonson's epithalamium in *The Underwood*,[7] which may well be influenced by *Epithalamion*, contains twenty-four stanzas similar in structure to Spenser's and covering the day and night of the marriage, the approximate date of which is referred to in the poem. But beyond this I find no signs in Jonson's poem of a complex symbolism of the kind sought. Many English epithalamia resemble Spenser's in all the respects in which Jonson's does save the number of stanzas, just as, of course, all Renaissance epithalamia have certain standard features which *Epithalamion* exhibits.

It may be that in time many poems of the Renaissance will be discovered to possess a symbolism resembling that of *Epithalamion*. Until that happens, however, a certain color can be given to the theory that Spenser arrived at his conception independently, by a process similar to that by which he may have arrived at the particular mode of composition we know in *The Faerie Queene*. We believe that this latter process was dictated by a number of considerations: his experience of Italian epic, the inheritance of a

[6] Cf. J. A. S. McPeek, "The Major Sources of Spenser's *Epithalamion*," *Journal of English and Germanic Philology*, XXXV (1936), 183–213.

[7] *Ben Jonson*, ed. C. H. Herford and P. and E. Simpson (Oxford, 1941), VII, 225.

native allegorical tradition and a tradition of exegesis, the belief
that all great literature is allegorical. These considerations, partly
theoretical and applied with a striking literal-mindedness and strict-
ness, operated together with a native bent to produce a kind of
allegorical narrative, for many of the characteristics of which it
is difficult to find an analogue before Spenser. Perhaps something
of the same kind came into operation in the creation of *Epithalamion.* One of the theoretical requirements for the epithalamium as
expressed by Scaliger [8] is striking in this connection, for it might
serve as an epigraph to Spenser's poem. In the process of offering
very full advice to the poet on what is to be included in the epithalamium as a form, Scaliger remarks that the writer of such a poem
must describe the qualities love and friendship as derived from the
first beginnings of the universe, and continues:

Qua tempestate post digestum Chaos, Caeli terraeque sunt nuptiae cele-
bratae. Quorum coniunctione & tunc species omnes productae sunt: &
ad eorum imitationem generando propagatae: ut quod materia prohibebat,
formarum ordinata successio adipisceretur immortalitatem.

What this amounts to is that Scaliger is requiring the epithalamial
poet to treat of how, at the beginning of the world, the nuptials
of heaven and earth were celebrated, by whose union all species of
things were brought forth, and by imitation of whom these species
propagated by generation, to the end that what is denied them by
the nature of their matter—namely immortality—might be attained by the ordered succession of their forms. The thought, of
course, is quite central to Spenser; it may be that long rumination
on the fitness of such an injunction as Scaliger's led this eclectically
philosophical, vastly syncretic, and literal-minded poet through the
incubation and to the final hatching of his astounding symbolism in

[8] *Julii Caesaris Scaligeri . . . Poetices libri septem . . . apud Petrum
Santandreanum* (1594), 3.101 (pp. 382–83). The treatment of the epi-
thalamium in George Puttenham, *The Arte of English Poesie,* ed. G. D.
Willcock and A. Walker (Cambridge, 1936), does not include this idea.

Epithalamion. All the same, one suspects that he may have had some more definite lead.

Unlike this startling technique, the thought which it embodies and the allegorical mode according to which it works will come as no great surprise to those who know Spenser, for the continuity with his thought and allegorical method in *The Faerie Queene* is easily seen. In terms of thought the resemblance to the Mutability Cantos is the most obvious, but just as important is that to the speculations about generation and the generations in the Garden of Adonis and the rest of Book III of *The Faerie Queene* at large; brings in time can achieve permanence only by constant renewal, according to Nature's plan. Adonis,

> All be he subject to mortalitie
> Yet is eterne in mutabilitie,
> And by succession made perpetuall.
>
> (3.6.47)

Furthermore, the gentle, fecund love in harmony of that Garden, as of the Venus of *Faerie Queene* 4.10.47 ("So all the world by thee at first was made,/ and dayly yet thou doest the same re-payre"), is far removed from the sterile pleasure of the once-born and soon dead rose—an emblem of mutability without cyclical recurrence—in the song for Acrasia (*Faerie Queene* 2.12.74–75) in the static and artificial Bower of Bliss, which embodies the self-defeating effort to create out of matter and time the kind of eternity proper only to spirit and God; and that love is equally far removed from the imperious Cupid, whose desire (like Dame Mutability's) is for unique mastery, not harmonious interplay, in the House of Busirane (*Faerie Queene* 3.12.22–23). Spenser's intentions here, and in the Mutability Cantos, very nearly mirror Chaucer's in *The Knight's Tale*, which makes the point more clearly: the love god ("The god of love, a, *benedicite!*") of The-seus' first extended speech there (ll. 1785–1825) exerts a fatal mastery over Palamon and Arcite; like a disease that can only be palliated, not cured, this runs its course and achieves its own quietus in Arcite's death. The harmony of Nature's universal plan, as expressed in Theseus' remarkable second declaration (ll. 2987–3093), then becomes operative, in a sense made clear in the Boethian source,[9] in the marriage of Palamon and Emily. These matters, and other analogues, have been touched on earlier in this book.

In terms of its allegorical mode, the demand that *Epithalamion* makes upon its reader is very much like the one made by *The Faerie Queene,* which is that several operations should be performed simultaneously. They may be reviewed here. Spenser asks us, first of all, to do what we have always done: to attend to the shimmering surface of his marriage day. But then he asks us to see operations proceeding integrally and at length beneath that dissolving surface. We are to think of the stanzas also as Hours, the apotheosis of the Hours that attend the bride and give her all that time can give. As well as on earth, they are in the heavens, and we are to think of each Hour in her poetic relation to her sister directly opposite her across the universe. One may be in light, the other may be in darkness; one prepares the chariot and horses of Phoebus each year for a space; the opposite one does the same six months later, so that in a sense they—the Horae—may be called daughters of Horus, the Egyptian god of the sun, attending him one at a time in his daily journeys until by the end of the year each of them has served him. We are asked to remember at each of the two great divisions of the poem two of the seasonal points, the positions of the heavens, the periods of light and darkness in which these Hours and their accompanying heavenly bodies participate, with all the "powers which in the same remayne." We must think of the substance of the poem as the substance of time itself—duration with its divisions—and we must see a year as a day, as God does. Finally we must see how man and the universe mirror

[9] *De consolatione philosophiae* 2. Met. 8.24–25, *passim.*

each other, and what paradoxical boon is granted to all of us: that though we may not endure individually, our mortality and the insufficiency of all created things is, by grace, only one aspect of a total situation of which cyclical return is the other face, until such time as time shall cease.

It goes without saying that here is not the place for the final word on the aesthetic success with which these demands are attended, because it is here that it is first claimed they are made at all. But, granted that Spenser makes them, it must be admitted, conditionally, that many a modern reader will still prefer to follow an orchestration of our sense of mortality and of our paradoxical defenses against time in more direct terms—in those of Shakespeare's sonnets, for instance—if, indeed, the reader does not feel, *tout court,* that any effort to orchestrate a defense against mortality is simply a bland attempt to insulate us against the truth of experience. But leaving out of the debate those of this latter persuasion (this is not the place to speak to their condition), it may still be pointed out that *Epithalamion* is in a sense one of the last great monuments to a mode of literary composition dominant through three centuries, just as it is one of the last great literary monuments of microcosmic-macrocosmic vision. It may be doubted that all the poets of those centuries were absolutely wrong in their choice of mode, or that the direct and forceful presentation of emotion in the sense in which Shakespeare presents it to us constitutes aesthetically the correction of a historically conditioned error of literary judgment, true as it is that the mode of the late Elizabethan and Jacobean lyricists is an addition to our store of expressive means. The mode which Spenser follows requires before everything else a pursuit of an integral meaning, integrally expressed, below the surface of discourse: whatever the inspired interplay may be by which the guidelines of one level of discourse are given by or related to another, and however strongly the poignancy in their mutually enforcing relation may speak to the heart, the direct bodying forth of meaning through imagery (which is a large part of Shakespeare's way of achieving lyrical effect) is denied in this mode, because its effect—the glamour or the awe it evokes—is so strongly dependent upon the fact of covertness itself. In the most general sense the method that Spenser follows belongs to a different sort of literature, well represented in other times and places—a kind in which an unexpected nexus of meaning, gradually intuited through large-scale effort, becomes a permanent and aesthetically valid possession for all readers.

Epithalamion

The text follows the Variorum Spenser, except that *i*, *u*, and *v* are normalized. On the left, plain numbering applies to the long lines, italics to the short lines. The usual line-numbering appears on the right.

Stanzas 1–12 are given opposite stanzas 13–24 so as to show the pairing described in Chapter II. Each of the odd-numbered stanzas occupies a verso page, and each of the even-numbered stanzas a facing recto. A description of the claimed or suspected points of correspondence appears in schematic form below each stanza, and is alphabetically keyed to the corresponding points in the description below the matching stanza on the facing page. The most likely points of correspondence are generally listed first; these are followed (in several cases accompanied) by other points which seem to me doubtful in varying degrees. These doubtful points have been italicized. Their inclusion does not imply that I wish to support their validity in every case; I have included them because I believe that we should consider possibilities beyond one person's judgment of likelihoods in the work of a poet whose multiple allusiveness and depth of covert reference still remain to be gauged. In every case the italics signify my doubt (in some cases very considerable doubt) as to the validity of the correspondence itself, but not as to the correctness of the datum upon which the suspicion of correspondence rests. The spelling of quotations from *Epithalamion* in the glosses is modernized. Line references are to the usual line-numbering. Authority for many of the claims of correspondence is given in Chapter II, which for the sake of clarity should be perused before, or in conjunction with, the following annotations.

The reader is reminded that the pairing is most obvious from stanzas 5 and 17 onward, from which point Spenser is in a position to play on day and night. Before that point the correspondences are generally more occult.

I.

1	Ye learned sisters which have oftentimes	
2	Beene to me ayding, others to adorne:	
3	Whom ye thought worthy of your gracefull rymes,	
4	That even the greatest did not greatly scorne	
5	To heare theyr names sung in your simple layes,	5

1   But joyed in theyr prayse

6	And when ye list your owne mishaps to mourne	
7	Which death, or love, or fortunes wreck did rayse,	
8	Your string could soone to sadder tenor turne,	
9	And teach the woods and waters to lament	10

2   Your doleful dreriment.

10	Now lay those sorrowful complaints aside,	
11	And having all your heads with girland crownd,	
12	Helpe me mine owne loves prayses to resound,	
13	Ne let the same of any be envide:	15

3   So Orpheus did for his own bride,

14	So I unto my selfe alone will sing,
15	The woods shall to me answer and my Eccho ring.

a. The Muses have honored the greatest in Spenser's poetry (1–6).
b. They are now to change their subject and, at the direction of the poet, sing the praises of his bride (12–14).
c. *The Muses aid the poet* (1–2).
d. *The poet will sing the praises of his love* (14–18).
e. *Orpheus sang of his own bride (to the powers of hell, so as to recover her); Spenser will sing her praises to himself (16–17).*

13.

187 Behold whiles she before the altar stands
188 Hearing the holy priest that to her speakes
189 And blesseth her with his two happy hands   225
190 How the red roses flush up in her cheekes,
191 And the pure snow with goodly vermill stayne,
37   Like crimsin dyde in grayne,
192 That even th'angels which continually,
193 About the sacred Altare doe remaine,   230
194 Forget their service and about her fly,
195 Ofte peeping in her face that seems more fayre,
38   The more they on it stare.
196 But her sad eyes still fastened on the ground,
197 Are governed with goodly modesty,   235
198 That suffers not one looke to glaunce awry,
199 Which may let in a little thought unsownd.
200 Why blush ye love to give to me your hand,
39   The pledge of all our band?
201 Sing ye sweet Angels, Alleluya sing,   240
202 That all the woods may answere and your eccho ring.

a. The angels are in the service of the Greatest around the altar (229–31).
b. They now forget their usual service and fly about the bride (231–33).
   The poet asks them to sing "alleluya" (240).
c. *The angels aid the priest* (229–30).
d. *The priest blesses the bride with his happy hands* (225).
e. *Spenser's bride will not turn her eyes aside to let in "a little thought un-
   sound"* (234–37); *Orpheus lost his bride by doing just this. Cf. Christian
   allegorical interpretation of the myth: Boethius,* De consolatione, *III, Met.
   12; Robert Henryson,* Orpheus and Eurydice, *ll. 415–60, 571–633.*

2.

16   Early before the worlds light giving lampe,
17   His golden beame upon the hils doth spred,   20
18   Having disperst the nights unchearefull dampe,
19   Doe ye awake, and with fresh lusty hed,
20   Go to the bowre of my beloved love,
4   My truest turtle dove,
21   Bid her awake; for Hymen is awake,   25
22   And long since ready forth his maske to move,
23   With his bright Tead that flames with many a flake,
24   And many a bachelor to waite on him,
5   In theyr fresh garments trim.
25   Bid her awake therefore and soone her dight,   30
26   For lo the wished day is come at last,
27   That shall for al the paynes and sorrowes past,
28   Pay to her usury of long delight:
6   And whylest she doth her dight,
29   Doe ye to her of joy and solace sing,   35
30   That all the woods may answer and your eccho ring.

a. *The action of the marriage begins* (22).
b. Hymen is awake and ready to set his masque into action, *with its trim bachelors* (26-29).

c. The wished-for day has come at last, which will bring long delight in place of past pains and sorrows (31-33).

d. *The muses are asked to sing of joy and solace* (35).

e. *The sun is to disperse the damp of night* (21).

14.

203	Now al is doen; bring home the bride againe,	
204	Bring home the triumph of our victory,	
205	Bring home with you the glory of her gaine,	
206	With joyance bring her and with jollity.	245
207	Never had man more joyfull day than this,	
40	Whom heaven would heape with blis.	
208	Make feast therefore now all this live long day,	
209	This day for ever to me holy is,	
210	Poure out the wine without restraint or stay,	250
211	Poure not by cups, but by the belly full,	
41	Poure out to all that wull,	
212	And sprinkle all the postes and wals with wine,	
213	That they may sweat, and drunken be withall.	
214	Crowne ye God Bacchus with a coronall,	255
215	And Hymen also crowne with wreathes of vine,	
216	And let the Graces daunce unto the rest;	
42	For they can doo it best:	
217	The whiles the maydens doe theyr carroll sing,	259
218	To which the woods shall answer and theyr eccho ring.	

a. *"Now all is done": the marriage is completed* (242).

b. Hymen (who does not appear elesewhere in the action, although he is prayed to in stanza 22) is to be crowned with wreaths, and so is Bacchus (*pun on Bacchus*) (255–56).

c. The joyful and holy day is celebrated (246–49) (no other discussions of the "day" are of comparable length and importance in the poem, except for the one in stanza 15, where the discussion is continued from stanza 14, and where it is necessary to make the point about St. Barnabas' Day).

d. *The Graces are asked to dance and the maidens to sing their carol* (257–59).

e. *Dampness is reestablished by the sprinkling of wine on the posts and walls so that they may "sweat"* (253–54).

3.

31   Bring with you all the Nymphes that you can heare
32   Both of the rivers and the forrests greene:
33   And of the sea that neighbours to her neare,
34   Al with gay girlands goodly wel beseene.   40
35   And let them also with them bring in hand
7   Another gay girland
36   For my fayre love of lillyes and of roses,
37   Bound truelove wize with a blew silke riband.
38   And let them make great store of bridale poses,   45
39   And let them eeke bring store of other flowers
8   To deck the bridale bowers.
40   And let the ground whereas her foot shall tread,
41   For feare the stones her tender foot should wrong
42   Be strewed with fragrant flowers all along,   50
43   And diapred lyke the discolored mead.
44   Which done, doe at her chamber dore awayt,
9   For she will waken strayt,
45   The whiles doe ye this song unto her sing,
46   The woods shall to you answer and your Eccho ring.   55

a.   The Muses are told to gather river- and forest-nymphs of the neighboring
      countryside, and sea-nymphs (apparently from the vicinity of Youghal,
      where the bride had been staying: see the Variorum note) (37–39);
      these are to perform duties in connection with the marriage (40–51).
b.   These duties are flower gathering and garlanding (40–51).

c.   The Muses are to sing *Epithalamion* (54).

d.   *The nymphs are to wear garlands and to bring another garland for the
      bride* (40–44). *These are presumably circular wreaths*

15.

219 Ring ye the bels, ye yong men of the towne,
220 And leave your wonted labors for this day:
221 This day is holy; doe ye write it downe,
222 That ye for ever it remember may.
223 This day the sunne is in his chiefest hight,   265
43 With Barnaby the bright,
224 From whence declining daily by degrees,
225 He somewhat loseth of his heat and light,
226 When once the Crab behind his back he sees.
227 But for this time it ill ordained was,   270
228 To chose the longest day in all the yeare,
229 And shortest night, when longest fitter weare:
230 Yet never day so long, but late would passe.
231 Ring ye the bels, to make it weare away,
44 And bonefiers make all day,   275
232 And daunce about them, and about them sing:
233 That all the woods may answer, and your eccho ring.

a. The young men of the town are to leave off their customary duties for
the day and perform activities in connection with the marriage (261–
64, 274–77).

b. This is St. Barnabas' Day (265–66), of which the chief popular activity is
garlanding with flowers. The young men's bell ringing and bonfires
(261, 274–76) may also have been associated in Spenser's mind or in
local custom with this day, but I find no indication of the usual association of these activities with St. Barnabas' Day; they are associated, rather,
with Midsummer Eve, which in late sixteenth-century England appears
to have been St. John's Eve, June 23.

c. The young men are to ring bells to make the day wear away (261, 274);
this may be associated with the Muses' singing of *Epithalamion*: the refrain ending the stanza hours concludes with the word "ring," and this
stanza also begins with this word, as though to emphasize the association;
twenty-three of the twenty-four stanzas thus wear the day away.

d. *The young men are to dance around bonfires (275–76). Presumably they
dance in a ring. It is barely possible that this is an allusion to the ring
of the Hours.*

4.

47   Ye Nymphes of Mulla which with carefull heed,
48   The silver scaly trouts doe tend ful well,
49   And greedy pikes which use therein to feed,
50   (Those trouts and pikes all others do excell)
51   And ye likewise which keepe the rushy lake,   60
10   Where none doo fishes take,
52   Bynd up the locks the which hang scatterd light,
53   And in his waters which your mirror make,
54   Behold your faces as the christall bright,
55   That when you come whereas my love doth lie,   65
11   No blemish she may spie.
56   And eke ye lightfoot mayds which keepe the deere,
57   That on the hoary mountayne use to towre,
58   And the wylde wolves which seeke them to devoure,
59   With your steele darts doo chace from comming neer, 70
12   Be also present heere,
60   To helpe to decke her and to help to sing,
61   That all the woods may answer and your eccho ring.

a. The nymphs of the river Mulla, who care for the trout and pike (fish
   that "excell" [59] all others elsewhere of the same varieties) are called
   upon, as well as the nymphs of the lake where there are no fish (56–61)

b. *The nymphs are to look at their reflections in the water* (63–64).

c. Their countenances are "crystal bright" (64) ; their locks "hang scattered
   light" (62).
d. *The maids who kept the deer on the mountains and protect them with
   steel darts against the ravening wolves are also called upon* (67–71).

16.

234	Ah when will this long weary day have end,	
235	And lende me leave to come unto my love?	
236	How slowly do the houres theyr numbers spend?	280
237	How slowly does sad Time his feathers move?	
238	Hast thee O fayrest Planet to thy home	
45	Within the Westerne fome:	
239	Thy tyred steedes long since have need of rest.	
240	Long though it be, at last I see it gloome,	285
241	And the bright evening star with golden creast	
46	Appeare out of the East.	
242	Fayre childe of beauty, glorious lampe of love	
243	That all the host of heaven in rankes doost lead,	
244	And guydest lovers through the nights dread,	290
245	How chearefully thou lookest from above,	
246	And seemst to laugh atweene thy twinkling light	
47	As joying in the sight	
247	Of these glad many which for joy doe sing,	
248	That all the woods them answer and their echo ring. 295	

a. The planet Venus, whose exaltation is in the zodiacal sign of the fish (*association between "excel" and "exaltation"*), and who is born from the water and associated with fish, becomes visible in the evening sky in the east, as the sun descends in the west (282–87). This is an astronomical impossibility, since she appears in the eastern sky only as a morning star. Spenser might have thought that by thus locating her, he was placing her in the zodiacal sign of Pisces, but it seems best to suppose that he had something else in mind here. Pisces is still below the eastern horizon when the sun is about to go down in the sign of Cancer (as here).

b. *Venus, leader of the hosts of heaven, looks down joyfully at the hosts of merry-makers below (291–94), who are all under the influence of the bride. Perhaps Venus sees in the bride a reflection of herself (cf. stanza 6).*

c. "Golden crest" (286), cheerful countenance (291), "twinkling light" (292) of Venus appear (rays of light are often compared to hair).

d. *Phoebus (282) protects various animals against the wolf; he is a protector of deer. Phoebus chasing away the wolf is said to be the sun dispelling pestilence or winter (the steel darts as rays of the sun).*

5.

62 Wake, now my love, awake; for it is time,
63 The Rosy Morne long since left Tithones bed,   75
64 All ready to her silver coche to clyme,
65 And Phoebus gins to shew his glorious hed.
66 Hark how the cheerefull birds do chaunt theyr laies
13   And carroll of loves praise.
67 The merry Larke her mattins sings aloft,   80
68 The thrush replyes, the Mavis descant playes,
69 The Ouzell shrills, the Ruddock warbles soft,
70 So goodly all agree with sweet consent,
14   To this dayes merriment.
71 Ah my deere love why doe ye sleepe thus long,   85
72 When meeter were that ye should now awake,
73 T'awayt the coming of your joyous make,
74 And hearken to the birds lovelearned song,
15   The deawy leaves among.
75 For they of joy and pleasance to you sing,   90
76 That all the woods them answer and theyr eccho ring.

a. The bride is asked to awaken since Aurora has left Tithonus' bed (74–75).
b. The sun begins to show "his glorious head" (77).
c. "Why do ye sleep thus long,/ When meeter were that ye should now awake" (85–86).
d. The stanza is like a medieval spring opening connoting May: the "love-learned" singing of the birds (78–83, 88), the morning (75), the sun (77) (cf. injunction to Spring in *Amoretti* 70 to go to the poet's love, "Yet in her winters bowre not well *awake*"; cf. also Spring and birds in *Amoretti* 19, and particularly the semi-Chaucerian passage in *Faerie Queene* 4.10.45, with its birds who are pages of Venus and are first to feel her influence in the spring and to express it through song)
e. "*the dewy leaves among*" (89).
f. *The birds sing* (78–83, 88).

17.

249 Now cease ye damsels your delights forepast;
250 Enough is it, that all the day was youres:
251· Now day is doen, and night is nighing fast:
252 Now bring the Bryde into the brydall boures.
253 Now night is come, now soone her disaray,   300
48 And in her bed her lay;
254 Lay her in lillies and in violets,
255 And silken courteins over her display,
256 And odourd sheets, and Arras coverlets.
257 Behold how goodly my faire love does ly   305
49 In proud humility;
258 Like unto Maia, when as Jove her tooke,
259 In Tempe, lying on the flowry gras,
260 Twixt sleepe and wake, after she weary was,
261 With bathing in the Acidalian brooke.   310
262 Now it is night, ye damsels may be gon,
50 And leave my love alone,
263 And leave likewise your former lay to sing:
264 The woods no more shall answere, nor your echo ring.

a. The damsels are asked to disarray and bed the bride (300–1).
b. Day is done and night is nighing fast (251); night has come (300).
c. Jove took Maia " 'Twixt sleep and wake" (307–9) (the verbatim parallel "sleep," "wake").
d. Maia (307) is the goddess of spring and of May; her name is etymologically related to that of the month.

e. *"The flowery grass"* (308); *"lilies and violets"* (302).
f. *The damsels are to stop singing* (313).

6.

77 My love is now awake out of her dreames,
78 And her fayre eyes like stars that dimmed were
79 With darksome cloud, now shew theyr goodly beames
80 More bright than Hesperus his head doth rere.   95
81 Come now ye damzels, daughters of delight, ˅
16   Helpe quickly her to dight,
82 But first come ye fayre houres which were begot
83 In Joves sweet paradice, of Day and Night,
84 Which doe the seasons of the yeare allot,   100
85 And al that ever in this world is fayre
17   Doe make and still repayre.
86 And ye three handmayds of the Cyprian Queene,
87 The which doe still adorne her beauties pride,
88 Helpe to addorne my beautifullest bride: 105
89 And as ye her array, still throw betweene
18   Some graces to be seene,
90 And as ye use to Venus, to her sing,
91 The whiles the woods shal answer and your eccho ring.

a. The bride's eyes, formerly dimmed like stars covered with dark clouds,
   now reveal their beams more brightly than the evening star, Hesper (93–
   95).
b. The Hours were begotten of Day and Night, in Jove's paradise (98–99)

c. The Hours and Graces are to adorn the bride (96–105).

18.

265	Now welcome night, thou night so long expected,	315
266	That long daies labour doest at last defray,	
267	And all my cares, which cruell love collected,	
268	Hast sumd in one, and cancelled for aye:	
269	Spread thy broad wing over my love and me,	
51	That no man may us see,	320
270	And in thy sable mantle us enwrap,	
271	From feare of perrill and foule horror free.	
272	Let no false treason seeke us to entrap,	
273	Nor any dread disquiet once annoy	
52	The safety of our joy:	325
274	But let the night be calme and quietsome,	
275	Without tempestuous storms or sad afray:	
276	Lyke as when Jove with fayre Alcmena lay,	
277	When he begot the great Tirynthian Groome:	
278	Or lyke as when he with thy selfe did lie,	330
53	And begot Majesty.	
279	And let the mayds and yongmen cease to sing:	
280	Ne let the woods them answer, nor theyr eccho ring.	

a. The wing of Night is to be spread over the bridal pair, and they are to be wrapped in her mantle; they will be invisible (319–21).

b. Majesty was begotten of Jove on Night (330–31), and Jove and Day are elsewhere equated in Spenser's work (cf. Chap. II); *Alcmene coupled with Jove (Day)* (328), *but also with Rhadamanthys (Night)*.

c. Night is to wrap the bridal pair in her mantle and cover them with her wing (319–21).

7.

92	Now is my love all ready forth to come,	110
93	Let all the virgins therefore well awayt,	
94	And ye fresh boyes that tend upon her groome	
95	Prepare your selves; for he is comming strayt,	
96	Set all your things in seemely good aray	
19	Fit for so joyfull day,	115
97	The joyfulst day that ever sunne did see.	
98	Faire Sun, shew forth thy favorable ray,	
99	And let thy lifull heat not fervent be	
100	For feare of burning her sunshyny face,	
20	Her beauty to disgrace.	120
101	O fayrest Phoebus, father of the Muse,	
102	If ever I did honour thee aright,	
103	Or sing the thing, that mote they mind delight,	
104	Doe not thy servants simple boone refuse,	
105	But let this day let this one day be myne,	125
21	Let all the rest be thine.	
106	Then I thy soverayne prayses loud wil sing,	
107	That all the woods shal answer and theyr eccho ring.	

a. The sun is asked to shine favorably and not to burn the bride's face (117–19); Phoebus is asked to let this one day be the poet's (121–26).

b. "If ever I did honour thee aright,/ Or sing the thing, that mote thy mind delight" (122–23); "Then I thy sovereign praises loud will sing" (127): delightful poetry.

c. *The danger of fervent and burning sunshine* (118–19).

19.

281 Let no lamenting cryes, nor dolefull teares,
282 Be heard all night within nor yet without: 335
283 Ne let false whispers, breeding hidden feares,
284 Breake gentle sleepe with misconceived dout.
285 Let no deluding dreames, nor dreadful sights
54   Make sudden sad affrights;
286 Ne let housefyres, nor lightnings helpelesse harmes, 340
287 Ne let the Pouke, nor other evill sprights,
288 Ne let mischivous witches with theyr charmes,
289 Ne let hob Goblins, names whose sence we see not,
55   Fray us with things that be not.
290 Let not the shriech Oule, nor the Storke be heard: 345
291 Nor the night Raven that still deadly yels,
292 Nor damned ghosts cald up with mighty spels,
293 Nor griesly vultures make us once affeard:
294 Ne let th'unpleasant Quyre of Frogs still croking
56   Make us to wish theyr choking.   350
295 Let none of these theyr drery accents sing;
296 Ne let the woods them answer, nor theyr eccho ring.

a. Night is asked to prevent misfortunes and inconveniences on this night
(334–52).
b. "Let none of these their dreary accents sing" (351): horrid sounds.
Witches' charms (342), cries of screech owl and stork (345), "yells" of
raven (346), spells (347), croaking of frogs (349). *"Hobgoblins"*
(343) *and Phoebus of stanza 7* (121) *possibly relate to Gabriel Harvey's
stricture on an early version of* The Faerie Queene: *". . . and* Hobgoblin
runne away with the Garland from Apollo . . ." (*Three Proper, and
Wittie, Familiar Letters, in The Poetical Works of Edmund Spenser,* ed.
J. C. Smith and E. De Sélincourt [London, 1952], p. 628)
c. *House fires, lightning* (340).

8.

108	Harke how the Minstrels gin to shrill aloud	
109	Their merry Musick that resounds from far,	130
110	The pipe, the tabor, and the trembling Croud,	
111	That well agree withouten breach or jar.	
112	But most of all the Damzels doe delite,	
22	When they their tymbrels smyte,	
113	And thereunto doe daunce and carrol sweet,	135
114	That all the sences they doe ravish quite,	
115	The whyles the boyes run up and downe the street,	
116	Crying aloud with strong confused noyce,	
23	As if it were one voyce.	
117	Hymen io Hymen, Hymen they do shout,	140
118	That even to the heavens theyr shouting shrill	
119	Doth reach, and all the firmament doth fill,	
120	To which the people standing all about,	
121	As in approvance doe thereto applaud	
24	And loud advaunce her laud,	145
122	And evermore they Hymen Hymen sing,	
123	That al the woods them answer and theyr eccho ring.	

a. Noise: minstrels, echoing music, pipe, tabor, fiddle, timbrel-smiting damsels, caroling (129–35); boys shouting "Hymen, io Hymen," so that shouting fills firmament (137–42); applause, singing (143–47).

b. Boys running up and down the street, shouting "Hymen, io Hymen" (137–40).

20.

297	But let stil Silence trew night watches keepe,	
298	That sacred peace may in assurance rayne,	
299	And tymely sleep, when it is tyme to sleepe,	355
300	May poure his limbs forth on your pleasant playne,	
301	The whiles an hundred little winged loves,	
57	Like divers fethered doves,	
302	Shall fly and flutter round about your bed,	
303	And in the secret darke, that none reproves,	360
304	Their prety stealthes shal worke, and snares shal spread	
305	To filch away sweet snatches of delight,	
58	Conceald through covert night.	
306	Ye sonnes of Venus, play your sports at will,	
307	For greedy pleasure, carelesse of your toyes,	365
308	Thinks more upon her paradise of joyes,	
309	Then what ye do, albe it good or ill.	
310	All night therefore attend your merry play,	
59	For it will soone be day:	
311	Now none doth hinder you, that say or sing,	370
312	Ne will the woods now answer, nor your Eccho ring.	

a. Silence, sacred peace, sleep (353–56).

b. Sons of Venus flying and fluttering around the bed, working their pretty
stealths and attending their merry play (357–64, 368) (cf. similar contrast in *Faerie Queene* 4.10.42.2–5).

9.

124   Loe where she comes along with portly pace
125   Lyke Phoebe from her chamber of the East,
126   Arysing forth to run her mighty race,   150
127   Clad all in white, that seemes a virgin best.
128   So well it her beseemes that ye would weene
25   Some angell she had beene.
129   Her long loose yellow locks lyke golden wyre,
130   Sprinkled with perle, and perling flowres a tweene,   155
131   Doe lyke a golden mantle her attyre,
132   And being crowned with a girland greene,
26   Seeme lyke some mayden Queene.
133   Her modest eyes abashed to behold
134   So many gazers, as on her do stare,   160
135   Upon the lowly ground affixed are.
136   Ne dare lift up her countenance too bold,
137   But blush to heare her prayses sung so loud,
27   So farre from being proud.
138   Nathlesse do ye still loud her prayses sing,   165
139   That all the woods may answer and your eccho ring.

a. The bride comes forth like the moon from the eastern horizon, to run
   her race in the skies; she is described in accordance with this conceit
   (148–58).
b. She seems like a maiden queen (158).

c. *She modestly lowers her eyes and blushes to hear her praises, which*
   nevertheless the poet commands to be continued (159–66)
d. Her eyes are fixed on the lowly ground (159–61).

21.

313 Who is the same, which at my window peepes?
314 Or whose is that faire face, that shines so bright,
315 Is it not Cinthia, she that never sleepes,
316 But walkes about high heaven al the night?   375
317 O fayrest goddesse, do thou not envy
60   My love with me to spy:
318 For thou likewise didst love, though now unthought,
319 And for a fleece of woll, which privily,
320 The Latmian shephard once unto thee brought,   380
61   His pleasures with thee wrought.
321 Therefore to us be favorable now;
322 And sith of wemens labours thou hast charge,
323 And generation goodly dost enlarge,
324 Encline thy will t'effect our wishful vow,   385
325 And the chast wombe informe with timely seed,
62   That may our comfort breed:
326 Till which we cease our hopefull hap to sing,
327 Ne let the woods us answere, nor our Eccho ring.

a. The moon with her fair face peeps in the window; she walks about heaven all the night (372–75).

b. The Virgin Queen, Cynthia, Elizabeth I, is alluded to, as has long been recognized (376–78, 382) (cf. the three Elizabeths—Spenser's queen, bride, and mother: *Amoretti* 74).

c. *Do not envy the bride* (376–77).

d. The moon looks down on the earth (372–73).

10.

140   Tell me ye merchants daughters did ye see
141   So fayre a creature in your towne before?
142   So sweet, so lovely, and so mild as she,
143   Adornd with beautyes grace and vertues store,   170
144   Her goodly eyes lyke Saphyres shining bright,
28   Her forehead yvory white,
145   Her cheekes lyke apples which the sun hath rudded,
146   Her lips lyke cherryes charming men to byte,
147   Her brest like to a bowle of creame uncrudded,   175
29   Her paps lyke lyllies budded,
148   Her snowie necke lyke to a marble towre,
149   And all her body like a pallace fayre,
150   Ascending uppe with many a stately stayre,
151   To honors seat and chastities sweet bowre.   180
152   Why stand ye still ye virgins in amaze,
30   Upon her so to gaze,
153   Whiles ye forget your former lay to sing,
154   To which the woods did answer and your eccho ring.

a. The physical beauties of the bride (167–84); "chastity's sweet bower"
   (180).

22.

328	And thou great Juno, which with awful might	390
329	The lawes of wedlock still dost patronize,	
330	And the religion of the faith first plight	
331	With sacred rites hast taught to solemnize:	
332	And eeke for comfort often called art	
63	Of women in their smart,	395
333	Eternally bind thou this lovely band,	
334	And all thy blessings unto us impart.	
335	And thou glad Genius, in whose gentle hand,	
336	The bridale bowre and geniall bed remaine,	
64	Without blemish or staine,	400
337	And the sweet pleasures of theyr loves delight	
338	With secret ayde doest succour and supply,	
339	Till they bring forth the fruitfull progeny,	
340	Send us the timely fruit of this same night.	
341	And thou fayre Hebe, and thou Hymen free,	405
65	Grant that it may so be.	
342	Til which we cease your further prayse to sing,	
343	Ne any woods shal answer, nor your Eccho ring.	

a. The use to which this body is to be put. The physical aspect of conception and issue: Juno (390, 394–95), Genius (398), Hebe, Hymen (405); prayer that conception may take place (404–6); the secret succoring of the pleasures of love (401–2).

11.

155	But if ye saw that which no eyes can see,	185
156	The inward beauty of her lively spright,	
157	Garnisht with heavenly guifts of high degree,	
158	Much more then would ye wonder at that sight,	
159	And stand astonisht lyke to those which red	
31	Medusaes mazeful hed.	190
160	There dwels sweet love and constant chastity,	
161	Unspotted fayth and comely womanhed,	
162	Regard of honour and mild modesty,	
163	There vertue raynes as Queene in royal throne,	
32	And giveth lawes alone.	195
164	The which the base affections doe obay,	
165	And yeeld theyr services unto her will,	
166	Ne thought of thing uncomely ever may	
167	Thereto approch to tempt her mind to ill.	
168	Had ye once seene these her celestial threasures,	200
33	And unrevealed pleasures,	
169	Then would ye wonder and her prayses sing,	
170	That al the woods should answer and your echo ring.	

a. The spiritual excellences of the bride (185–203).

b. These are "heavenly" (187) and "celestial" (200).

c. They are invisible (185), inward (186), unrevealed (201)

23.

344 And ye high heavens, the temple of the gods,
345 In which a thousand torches flaming bright   410
346 Doe burne, that to us wretched earthly clods,
347 In dreadful darknesse lend desired light; .
348 And all ye powers which in the same remayne,
66   More than we men can fayne,
349 Poure out your blessing on us plentiously,   415
350 And happy influence upon us raine,
351 That we may raise a large posterity,
352 Which from the earth, which they may long possesse,
67   With lasting happinesse,
353 Up to your haughty pallaces may mount,   420
354 And for the guerdon of theyr glorious merit
355 May heavenly tabernacles there inherit,
356 Of blessed Saints for to increase the count.
357 So let us rest, sweet love, in hope of this,
358 And cease till then our tymely joyes to sing,   425
359 The woods no more us answer, nor our eccho ring.

a. An appeal for spiritual excellences in the offspring; after felicity on earth, a saintly place in Heaven (409–23).
b. The high heavens, temple of the gods (409); the light of the stars given to benighted humanity as a revelation of spiritual order (410–12).
c. The powers of the heavenly bodies are beyond man's insight (413–14).

12.

171	Open the temple gates unto my love,	
172	Open them wide that she may enter in,	205
173	And all the postes adorne as doth behove, .	
174	And all the pillours deck with girlands trim,	
175	For to recyve this Saynt with honour dew,	
34	That cometh in to you.	
176	With trembling steps and humble reverence,	210
177	She commeth in, before the almighties vew:	
178	Of her ye virgins learne obedience,	
179	When so ye come into those holy places,	
35	To humble your proud faces;	
180	Bring her up to th'high altar that she may	215
181	The sacred ceremonies there partake,	
182	The which do endlesse matrimony make,	
183	And let the roring Organs loudly play	
184	The praises of the Lord in lively notes,	
36	The whiles with hollow throates	220
185	The Choristers the joyous Antheme sing,	
186	That al the woods may answere and their eccho ring.	

a. "Due" (208), "endless" (217).

b. The temple gates are to be opened wide, the posts are to be adorned (206), the pillars are to be decked (207) to give due (208) honor to the bride.

c. The sacred ceremonies making endless matrimony (215–22), (the eternal nature of the sacrament, and perhaps the assurance of the continuance, by generation, of mortal man).

d. Awe before the Almighty (210–14).

24.

360 Song made in lieu of many ornaments,
361 With which my love should duly have bene dect,
362 Which cutting off through hasty accidents,
363 Ye would not stay your dew time to expect,   430
68   But promist both to recompens,
364 Be unto her a goodly ornament,
365 And for short time an endlesse moniment.

a. "Duly" (428), "due" (430), "endless" (433) (the words are used in the poem only in stanzas 12 and 24).
b. The bride should duly (428) have been decked (428) with many ornaments (427), for which this poem is a recompense. (In addition to the parallelism in thought, each of the words immediately followed by a line reference has its counterpart in the matching stanza.)
c. The endless monument made by this poem to short time (433) (the eternizing power of poetry over the temporal events which it celebrates).

d. The relation between time and Eternity (433).

APPENDIX: THE HOURS

Hoold thou thy pees, thou poete Marcian,
That writest us that ilke weddyng murie
Of hire Philologie and hym Mercurie,
And of the songes that the Muses songe!
To smal is bothe thy penne, and eek thy tonge,
For to descryven of this mariage.

(Merchant's Tale, ll. 1732–37)

In addition to the material collected in the notes of the Variorum
edition on Spenser's reference to the Hours in stanza 11, lines
98–102, and the other material cited in Chapter III above, further documentation is relevant. Classical references to the Hours
are collected in Pauly-Wissowa, *Real-Encyclopädie der classischen
Altertumswissenschaft* (art. "Horai"), and in Daremberg and
Saglio, *Dictionnaire des antiquités* (arts. "Horae," "Gratiae,"
"Dies"). The classical Hours are daughters of Jove and Themis
(not Day and Night) and, with the Graces, frequently attend
Venus. It is only by a late classical tradition that they are thought
of as diurnal or both diurnal and seasonal; mythologically and
poetically they had formerly represented only the seasons. Ovid
makes the daily Hours yoke the chariot of the sun (*Metamorphoses* 2.118–19) and attend on Phoebus at equal distances from
each other ("positae spatiis aeqdalibus Horae," *Metamorphoses*
2.26)—a reference to their position in the sky. Nonnus[1] makes
the circling Hours of the day (twelve, according to classical
usage), who are daughters of Chronos, visit the palace of their
father Helios, where reside another set of Hours representing

---

[1] *Dionysiaca,* 12.14 ff.

the seasons. The diurnal Hours [2] are said by him to be priestesses each in turn, which suggests their sidereal, not solar, motion. Quintus Smyrnaeus [3] gives us but one set of twelve circling Hours; they are the companions of the Dawn (and consequently diurnal) but they are also divided into companies to represent the seasons, again suggesting sidereal rather than solar significance. This seems close to Spenser's conception. Macrobius [4] derives *hora* in both its daily and seasonal significance from the name of Horus, the Egyptian Apollo. Boccaccio [5] reproduces this, and calls them daughters of the sun and Chronos; he thinks of them as created by a certain measurement of the sun's progress through the sky. The poetic fiction that the steeds and chariot of the sun are readied by the Hours he explains by saying that night falls and day approaches as the hours succeed each other, and that the sun advances through the sky by the succession of the hours; furthermore, he says, when the Hours are described as opening the gates of heaven for the sun, what is meant is that daybreak, or the ascent of the sun above the horizon, may be imagined as under the control of the appropriate Hour. Much of this material (though not that from Quintus Smyrnaeus and Nonnus) is reproduced [6] in later Renaissance reference works.

[2] These are taken by the author of the article "Horai" in Pauly-Wissowa to represent the months. They are more usually thought to signify the hours of the day. Cf. art. "Horae" in Daremberg and Saglio, and the note to the passage in the Loeb Classical Library edition (Cambridge, Mass., 1940).

[3] *The Fall of Troy*, 11.48 ff., 593 ff. Cf. Pauly-Wissowa, art. "Horai."

[4] *Saturnaliorum*, 1.21.

[5] *Genealogie deorum gentilium libri* (i.e., the *De genealogia deorum*), ed. V. Romano (Scrittori d'Italia, N. 200–201, Bari, 1951), I, 162.

[6] Natalis Comes, *Mythologiae, sive explicationum fabularum . . . Parisiis, apud Arnoldum Sittart . . .* , 1583, 3.16 (pp. 414–16). Charles Estienne, *Dictionarium historicum, geographicum, poeticum* (Oxford, 1670, art. Horae [this late edition was the only one available to me]). *Imagines deorum . . . olim a Vincentio Chartario . . . collectae . . . nunc . . . Latino sermone ab Antonio Verderio, Domino Vallisprivatae, . . . expressae . . . Lugduni,* 1581, art. "Gratiae." Other such books do not yield such extensive material as these.

In stanza 6 Spenser reverses the usual order and emphasis for the Graces and the Hours as attendants of Venus. Usually the Graces come first and are more important. But, even so, perhaps he imagined these two classes of beings as Cartari [7] (following Apuleius) describes them accompanying Venus at a wedding: "eam lascivi Amores praecedebant, faces praeferentes, ut antiquorum erat mos, apud quos quinque pueri novam sponsam, ad mariti domum euntem cum facibus praecedebant. Veneris quoque latera hinc Gratiae, illinc Horae claudebant, quae floreis sertis voluptatum Deam adornare videbantur."

[7] *Imagines deorum* (as above), art. "Venus" (p. 344). A translation follows: "Before her [i.e., Venus in procession] went wanton loves bearing torches in accordance with the custom of the ancients. In their midst five boys with torches preceded the bride as she pursued her way to the house of the bridegroom. As in front, so on both sides Venus was attended—on the one side by the Graces, on the other by the Hours, both groups being seen to adorn with flowery garlands the goddess of delights."

INDEX

Alcmene, as parent of Hercules, 26, 97*n*; as wife of Rhadamanthys, 27, 97*n*

Amoretti (Spenser), 55, 71, quoted, 73

Apollo, as protector of animals, 25-26, 26*n*

Artemis cult, 26

Bennett, J. A. W., *The Parlement of Foules*, cited, 53

Berger, Harry, Jr., *The Allegorical Temper* . . . , quoted, 67*n*

Boccaccio, Giovanni, *Genealogie deorum gentilium libri*, cited, 112

Boethius, Anicius Manlius Severinus, *De consolatione philosophiae*, cited, 80, 87*n*, quoted, 53

Borders, ornamental, in first edition of *Amoretti and Epithalamion*, 73-74*n*

Bosanquet, Eustace F., *English Printed Almanacs and Prognostications . . . to the Year 1600*, quoted, 64*n*

Boyle, Elizabeth (Spenser's bride), 5

Brand, Ellis, *Observations on Popular Antiquities*, cited, 20*n*

Browne, Sir Thomas, quoted, 23

Buckminster, Thomas, 64*n*

Canzone, as model for *Epithalamion*, 44-46

Cartari, Vincent, *Imagines deorum* . . . , cited, 112*n*, quoted, 113

Caxton, William, *Mirrour of the World*, quoted, 37

Chaucer, Geoffrey, *The Knight's Tale*, 79-80, quoted, 52, 53; *The Merchant's Tale*, quoted, 111; *The Parlement of Foules*, cited, 53; *The Squire's Tale*, quoted, 23; *The Wife of Bath's Prologue*, quoted, 23

Curtius, E. R., *European Literature and the Latin Middle Ages*, cited, 76*n*

Dante Alighieri, *Divina Commedia*, 76, *Purgatorio*, cited, 24

Daphnaida (Spenser), 76

Day, as parent of Hours, 26-28, 96*n*; symbolized by stanzas of *Epithalamion*, 53

Donne, John, poetry of, 6-7; *A Nocturnal upon St. Lucy's Day*, cited, 40; *The Sun Rising*, quoted, 59

Du Bartas, Guillaume de Salluste, *La Première Sepmaine*, 75; *Les semaines*, 67

Du Bellay, Joachim, 67

"Due" ("dew"), 17, 47-50, 59, 108*n*, 109*n*

"Duly," 17, 47, 109*n*

Elizabeth I, 16, 103*n*

"Endlesse," 17, 47-48, 108*n*, 109*n*

Envoy to Ruines of Rome: by Bellay (Spenser), quoted, 8